Pure Joy

www.**transworldbooks**.co.uk

Also by Danielle Steel

* Published outside the UK under the title PASSION'S PROMISE

For more information on Danielle Steel and her books, see her
website at www.daniellesteel.com

DANIELLE STEEL

Pure Joy

BANTAM PRESS

LONDON · TORONTO · SYDNEY · AUCKLAND · JOHANNESBURG

TRANSWORLD PUBLISHERS
61–63 Uxbridge Road, London W5 5SA
A Random House Group Company
www.transworldbooks.co.uk

First published in the United States
in 2013 by Delacorte Press
an imprint of The Random House Publishing Group

First published in Great Britain
in 2013 by Bantam Press
an imprint of Transworld Publishers

A CIP catalogue record for this book
is available from the British Library.

ISBN 9780593071724

Addresses for Random House Group Ltd companies outside the UK
can be found at: www.randomhouse.co.uk
The Random House Group Ltd Reg. No. 954009

The Random House Group Limited supports the Forest Stewardship Council® (FSC®),
the leading international forest-certification organisation. Our books carrying the FSC
label are printed on FSC®-certified paper. FSC is the only forest-certification scheme
supported by the leading environmental organisations, including Greenpeace. Our
paper procurement policy can be found at www.randomhouse.co.uk/environment

Printed and bound in Great Britain by
CPI Group (UK) Ltd, Croydon, CR0 4YY

2 4 6 8 10 9 7 5 3 1

MIX
Paper from
responsible sources
FSC® C016897

To my beloved dog-loving and non-dog-loving children: Beatrix, Trevor, Todd, Nick, Sam, Victoria, Vanessa, Maxx, and Zara,

For all the good times we shared with our crazy and much-loved dogs, past and present;

So also to Simon, Tippy, Birdie, Pretzel, Tallulah, Gidget, Nancy, Minnie, Gracie, Ruby, Meg, and Hope.

And in loving memory of Jack, Roy, Ellie, Paddington, Tilly, Molly, Mia, Chiquita, Lola, Tiger Lily, Annabelle, Greta, Cookie, Licorice, Victoire, Oz, and somewhat grudgingly to Trixie and Sweet Pea.

To Cassio, who takes such incredible care of me, my family, and our dogs, with so much wisdom, dedication, and love.

To my wonderful friend Victoria Fay Leonard, who knows everything about dogs and gives the best advice.

To Alex, who loves Minnie too.

And to John, The Great Dog Lover who started it all,

with all my love,

d.s.

CONTENTS

*Minnie in the Paris apartment kitchen,
next to my desk, in her favorite bed*
Alessandro Calderano

FOREWORD

Minnie and Me

There have always been somewhat comedic aspects to my life, although sometimes I don't see it that way. A family of nine children, eleven dogs at one time, and a Vietnamese potbellied pig was bound to create some unusual situations, which even I found funny at the time. Someone once suggested a weekly TV series loosely based on our family, and we declined. Us? Funny? Of course not! Well . . . maybe a little. But it's only now, when thinking about these situations involving our dogs, that I realize how ridiculous some of them were.

Most of the children have grown up, the dogs we have now are divided between their homes and mine (I often babysit for my "grand dogs"), and we're down to more normal numbers. But it was only when a tiny eight-week-old, barely one-pound, long-haired white "teacup" Chihuahua snagged my heart that

I was inspired to write about her and share some of the other dog stories in my life. And just looking at her, you know she's a star. Her name is Minnie Mouse, and her favorite pose is lying in one of her pink beds, with her tiny paws crossed, looking at me with big brown eyes.

I never thought I'd fall in love with such a tiny dog. When one of my daughters got a Chihuahua in her early teens, I objected strenuously to having such a small dog. I thought people would step on her, something terrible would happen, she would be too fragile, I insisted that you can't have a dog that size. I discovered that despite her size, Chiquita, our first Chihuahua, was sturdy, had a big personality, and we only just lost her at sixteen. She was full of fun, healthy, and lively right to the end. She came to visit me regularly in San Francisco, after she and my daughter moved to Hollywood. Chiquita was a star!

But I still never thought the breed was for me. Whatever we decide we *don't* want in life (whether it's dating, houses, neighborhoods, jobs, partners, or dogs), the fates usually intervene to open our eyes and prove us wrong. So on a cold November day, at a pet store in New York, thinking myself hardened, sophisticated (and opinionated), I fell in love.

Two years later, the love affair is still going strong. The object of my affections is my now two-pound Chihuahua,

Minnie Mouse, who is the most adorable, lovable dog I've had yet. And the breed is even better than I thought. And she's taught me more about owning a dog than all the breeds that came before her. There's a reason why you see so many Chihuahuas on the street now (and cozily tucked away in apartments)—they are smart, fun, easy to take care of, and endearing in many ways. She warms my heart and makes me laugh.

While I turned down the weekly series about our family, all those years ago, I want to share with you all our slightly crazy and funny family dog stories, and tell you about Minnie and me and the practical things I've learned over the years about owning dogs.

As for Minnie, it is absolutely absurd that anything so small should own my heart, but she does. It just goes to show, never say never, or the next thing you know, you'll be doing what you said you never would, owning a dog you swore you didn't want and walking (or carrying) a tiny, totally enchanting little dog on a rhinestone-studded pink leash. You too could fall head over heels for a teacup Chihuahua, because owning a puppy, or a dog you love, is pure joy . . . that's what Minnie is for me!!!

love, d.s.

Pure Joy

Gidget

Danielle Steel

ONE

The Dog(s) and I

In the classic sense, I have never considered myself a "dog person," in that extreme way that some people are "dog" people, or "cat" people, or "horse" people, where they go to horse or dog shows, are obsessively dedicated to their animals, and know everything about the breeds. On the other hand, I'm definitely not a cat person, because I'm severely allergic to cats. When I was a child, about five or six years old, I used to visit the next-door neighbor's cats, and my eyes would swell until they almost closed, as tears streamed down my cheeks, my nose ran, and I couldn't breathe. If I stayed long enough, I had an asthma attack, and then I would go home wheezing and coughing and barely able to see, and my mother would say, "You went to visit the neighbor's cat again, didn't you?" Immediate look of innocence from me between wheezes: "Me? The cat? No . . . why?"

I finally stopped visiting the neighbor's cat, and my allergy has prevented me from really getting to know cats, so all the delightful things cat lovers say about them are unknown to me. And probably my most noteworthy cat encounter was at the home of Elizabeth Taylor. She contacted me years ago, to discuss writing a screen treatment for her. I was incredibly impressed and even more so when she invited me to her home. Nothing would have kept me from the opportunity to visit her. I was dying to meet the legend and see where she lived. I showed up for the meeting, and she was very nice. I was in awe of her, and we talked about some ideas, and as we did, a cat sauntered into the room, and I thought, "Oh no, this is not going to be good." Imagined or real, my eyes and nose began to itch instantly, and I said nothing and went on talking to her, just as another cat walked in. And within a few minutes, there were four or five cats wandering around the room. I started choking and knew I would have an asthma attack any minute.

I then made one of those major life decisions: was I going to admit to my frailties and run out the door, or stick it out so as not to lose this opportunity with an icon whom I had wanted to meet for years? I decided that even if I died in her living room, I didn't care. I stuck it out for as long as I could, eyes running, sneezing, and choking. I figured the meeting would end when she called 911, and I died of an asthma attack in her living room. By the time the meeting reached its conclusion, I could hardly breathe. The project went nowhere, but I got to spend an hour with a Hollywood legend. That was my last serious cat encounter. Since then, when I'm invited to someone's home, I ask if they have a cat. It makes me sound hopelessly neurotic but spares them the annoyance of having to call 911 half an hour after I get there. So cats just aren't part of the landscape for me.

Actually, I'm more of a "kid person," as witnessed by the fact that I have nine children. I can never resist a child, especially my own.

But dogs have been part of my life ever since I was a child. Some have been better than others and more memorable. Until recently, I never had a dog with a real nose. We had pugs when I was a child. My first dog was a fawn pug named James, and I adored him. Unfortunately, he died the same year my mother left, when I was six, which must have traumatized me, in both cases, because although I had other dogs after that, I never got seriously attached to another dog for many years, until I was an adult, even though there were always dogs in my life. And in a sense, I suppose I am a dog person because I like them. There are statues of dogs by assorted contemporary artists, in a multitude of colors, all over my Paris apartment.

My father continued to have pugs long after my favorite one died (of heat stroke, which was very sad). And after that dogs were not an important feature in my life for a while.

And then, as an adult, I decided to get a rescue dog, an adorable three-month-old basset hound puppy named Elmer (he came with the name). He was a "harlequin," so he was black and white, and he was one of the funniest dogs I ever had, and had a personality to go with the sad, droopy eyes. As a puppy, he would trot along and step on his ears with his big paws, which made him bonk his nose into the floor, and he would sit down and bark at me with an accusing look, as though I had tripped him, which I swear I didn't.

I had Elmer in my struggling days as a young writer, and my budget was pretty tight then. And Elmer's favorite trick was that he learned to operate the pedal that opened my refrigerator. I would come home from work (as an advertising copywriter) to find Elmer sprawled out in the kitchen, exhausted after eating everything in the fridge. I finally had to put a gate on the kitchen, or he would have eaten me out of house and home, but I loved him. Bassets are basically hunting dogs, so the minute you open a door, they take off like a shot. He ran away dozens of times, and I would find him halfway across town. Another not-so-charming trait is that they "bay," which is an agonizingly piercing howl, if you leave them alone for more than five seconds, which your neighbors will want to kill you for. I finally had to take him to work with me, because I couldn't leave him alone at home.

Despite his voracious appetite and the howling, I loved Elmer, and he was a very sweet dog. He slept on my bed, had no idea he was supposed to be a watchdog, and could have happily slept through a war. I don't think he knew he was a dog . . . until . . . a female basset came into his life, and everything changed. Peaceful, lazy, sleepy Elmer (who once ate an entire Gouda cheese, red wax and all, and had a stomachache for three days) suddenly woke up when he discovered the female sex!

My vet had a female basset he wanted to give up, and I agreed to try her for a weekend and see how they got along. I thought it might be nice for Elmer to have a friend. She was perfect for the entire weekend, impeccably behaved, and easy to have around. On Monday morning I called and agreed to adopt her. And by Monday night, her real personality emerged. Her name was Maude. She howled even louder than Elmer, was nervous and cranky, and a week later bit the neighbor's child. And her clever previous owner refused to take her back (he didn't think it would be good for her to be "rejected" for a second time . . . ugh . . . so I was stuck with her). She had to wear a muzzle, and overnight she turned Elmer into a dog, instead of the happy, easygoing guy he'd been before. Maude also had "issues," she had imaginary pregnancies several times a year. She would adopt one of my shoes as her "puppy," and try to bite me when I attempted to reclaim the shoe, which occasionally created a wardrobe crisis for me if she took over a shoe I needed for work or a date.

I kept the dogs as a pair for several years, but it was never a wonderful arrangement once Maude arrived. Together they were a powerful force, and once my daughter was old enough, she would walk them, while they pulled her down the street. She looked like Ben-Hur driving the chariot. Finally we all agreed that they needed a home in the country, and I found a family that was thrilled to have them. And I hate to say it, but I was relieved to see them go. They were a lot of work, and Elmer was never as sweet after Maude arrived. (Dogs sometimes act doggier when there is more than one of them.)

I was peacefully dogless then for a while and can't say I missed having a dog. Elmer and Maude had worn me out and took a lot of managing, between howling, running away, and eating everything in the house.

But when I married a man who was a serious dog person, dogs reentered my life en masse. He had a very old black miniature dachshund whom he adored, who had the incredibly bad timing to die during the weekend we got married, so my brand-new husband spent the day after the wedding crying and mourning his dog. This was not the happy scenario I'd had in mind, so I spent the next three days running around to breeders to find him a new dog, and I was thrilled to find a black miniature dachshund puppy who looked like the one he'd lost. (Fortunately we weren't planning to honeymoon for another month, so I had time to look for the dog.) She was a very sweet puppy, and I put her in a big blue Tiffany box that one of our wedding presents had come in and presented her to him that night. He was ecstatic and named her Sweet Pea. (Our nicknames for each other were Popeye and Olive, so she was our first "child.")

And in the ensuing months, Sweet Pea taught me a lot about co-owning a dog. According to John, she was half his and half mine. What I didn't know, when I made that deal, was that the front end was his and the back end was mine. She was very difficult to housebreak, and any "accidents" were my responsibility since the back end was mine. John had a rather creative way of draping paper towels over Sweet Pea's "mistakes," like flags, so I wouldn't miss them when I got home and had to clean them up. Owning her back end was not what I'd anticipated. Her front end wasn't so charming either, since she decided early on that she didn't like me (maybe for putting her in the Tiffany box, although it was only for five minutes for the presentation and to surprise John), and she snapped at me whenever she could. And when she slept in bed with us every night, she would sidle over to my side of the bed, pee, and then go back to John and snuggle up on the dry side. Sweet Pea and I had a somewhat rocky relationship after that.

Also, to a true dog lover, a really passionate one, their dog can do no wrong. (My father was one of those too. He had a dog that bit people regularly, and he always blamed the victim, not the dog.) In John's case, no matter what humor he was in, he was thrilled to see his dog. He would talk baby talk to her for hours and tell her how beautiful she was. Occasionally, confused, I would think he was talking to me, only to discover when I turned around that he was gazing into Sweet Pea's eyes. Okay, she was cute. But their love fests used to get on my nerves, and I had no dog of my own at the time. (But I couldn't imagine myself telling a dog how gorgeous he was, if I did. I mean after all, a dog is a dog . . . sometimes.) So Sweet Pea and I coexisted like two women in love with the same man, under one roof. And more often than I liked to admit, she won.

During and after Sweet Pea came a cavalcade of my children's dogs. True dog lover that he was, John felt that each child should have their own dog . . . wow!!! That got to be a *lot* of dogs, because we had a lot of kids. My oldest daughter, Beatrix, had acquired a Norwich terrier by then, named Jack. He was very cute and had a weakness for candy and bubble gum. He particularly loved Easter and Halloween when he would eat all the jellybeans and trick-or-treat candy. Bazooka bubble gum remained his drug of choice. (No, he did not blow bubbles out the other end, but he would look like a basketball after his raids, and it took a while for him to get back to normal again.) My two stepsons had two toy fox terriers, Paddington and Tilly. My son Nick had a miniature Brussels griffon (looks like an Ewok) named Molly. And when Sam got old enough, she got a black miniature dachshund of her own named Mia, who was incredibly mischievous and fortunately liked me a lot better than Sweet Pea did. Her weakness was for anything chocolate, which can be lethal to dogs. She would find it anywhere (particularly in my purse) and then have to be rushed to the vet to have her stomach pumped. Victoria had her tiny black teacup Chihuahua, Chiquita (whom Sam later adopted), that she carried everywhere. Vanessa had a very sweet miniature Yorkshire terrier, Lola, and later Gidget. And my youngest son, Maxx, had a miniature Boston bull, Annabelle, who was a truly great dog, and we all loved her. One word of warning about Boston bulls, though. They can jump to amazing heights and spring straight up off the ground. It took me months to figure out who was eating all the food we'd leave in bowls on the kitchen table. I finally saw one of her amazing Superman leaps and watched her land on the table with glee. Maxx's current Boston bull, Nancy, leaps straight from the floor into our arms with no warning, and then kisses the face of the astonished person holding her. They are an incredibly loving breed.

Fortunately, my youngest daughter, Zara, was so fed up with dogs, she didn't want one, which was an enormous relief. We had a house full of dogs, each with its own personality, as well as the traits of the breed. The kids were very good with them, responsible for them, but let's face it, that was a flock of dogs! And their father was teaching the children how important it was to love dogs, which was probably a valuable lesson, but it seemed like an army of dogs to me!

One thing that always fascinated me was that if one of the dogs made a "mistake" somewhere in the house, everyone always reported it to me—and I didn't even have a dog. I would call in whatever kids were around, since the problem had obviously been caused by one of their dogs, and I expected them to clean it up. The kids would then arrive on the scene, examine the problem intently, and announce, "It wasn't my dog." Excuse me? Do the dogs sign it or what? How do you *know* it wasn't your dog? Please! "Nope," the owner of the dog would say with absolute certainty. "I can tell, it wasn't my dog." *How* can you tell? You *cannot* tell, and since I didn't do it, one of their dogs did. We had some real battles over that, and no one *ever* confessed to their dog's mistakes. So either I'd have a fit and tell them to clean it up anyway (less often), or I'd just give up and clean it up myself (more often. I told you, I'm a total sucker for kids, even more than dogs). I will never understand how they could look me in the eye and say it wasn't their dog, but they did, regularly. The high (or low?) point of these disputes happened between my daughter Beatrix and son Todd, when each flatly refused to admit to their dog's guilt, and for once, I wouldn't back down. I told them to resolve the argument and clean it up! Their compromise solution was to get a disposable plastic knife and cut the "problem" in half. Each cleaned up half. Problem solved!

Other than that, all the kids and dogs got on very well. It made for an incredible scene when we left for the weekends in a stretch van with all nine kids, their backpacks, sports equipment, musical instruments, suitcases—and dogs. None of the dogs ever fought, and all were very sweet. The kids didn't fight much either, which is one of my theories about big families. With so many siblings to choose from, the dynamics of big families are fairly easy, and maybe the dogs proved that as well.

I took a slightly removed position about the dogs then. They were a sort of extension of the kids, and I had no particular preference or attachment to any of them. After all, they weren't mine—they belonged to John and the kids. So I felt responsible for them in a caretaking role but possessive about none of them. I had never really fallen in love with a dog since my very first one when I was six. And maybe his untimely death made me loath to get too attached to another dog myself. I hadn't really become a true dog person yet. (I should perhaps mention that John had also acquired a Vietnamese potbellied pig by then too, named Coco Chanel. We were promised that she would grow no larger than 35 pounds, but she made it to 250 pounds with ease. And let me tell you, that is one uncharming pet—their virtues are vastly overrated. The only amusing thing about her was that she had a vet named Dr. Bacon. Other than that, I did not enjoy her! So I am clearly not a pig person.)

I was happily rolling along, driving car pool, going to soccer games and ballet classes with the kids, shepherding my kids and their dogs, and writing books at night. Life seemed pretty simple then (to me, at least—I was used to the circus of our daily existence), and to be serious for a moment, they were the happiest years of my life and I knew it even then. I loved my big family and everything that went with it!!

One day John and I were browsing through an antique store, and the owner had a really sweet little dog, a small black miniature Brussels griffon. They have squashed-in faces and wiry coats and are really nice, very affectionate dogs. I admired the dog, said how cute she was, and we left. And the next day the antique dealer called me, sounding excited, and said, "She's on her way to you, she'll be here in two hours." Who will be here in two hours? I wasn't expecting anyone. He rapidly explained that his dog had a littermate, a sister, who had never found a home, came from Ohio, and he had had the breeder send her to me as a gift. *What?* Did I want a dog? *No!* Now what was I going to do? The dog was on a plane, on its way to me, and I thought it was an incredibly presumptuous thing to do. How could he send me a *dog* without even knowing if I wanted one? We already had a flock of dogs!

I was furious, but feeling somehow responsible for this unwanted gift, I went to the airport and picked up the dog, determined to give it to someone else or send it back. I picked up the crate and looked inside. The dog I had admired was small, cuddly, perfect, even beautiful. And when I opened the crate, I found myself looking at a gargoyle with fur. The poor thing looked at me with worried eyes. She was much bigger than her sister and noticeably overweight, and she had a massive underbite that made her look like a bulldog. It was a classic case of the beautiful sister (I had met) and the ugly one (I had just received). I felt so sorry for the dog, and she arrived with the name of Greta. But she was even sweeter than her sister. She looked embarrassed to be there, like an uninvited guest.

I took her home, and John laughed when he saw her and said, "Now there's a face only a mother could love," and I bristled. What a mean thing to say about my dog!! I had to take several of the kids to the orthodontist that afternoon, and took her with me, and the minute he saw her, the orthodontist looked at her with fascination. "Ah! She has a class-three malocclusion. If she were a human, I could fit her with braces for that." Great.

I don't know what happened, but beautiful or not, I fell in love with Greta that day. I had managed to avoid dog-love for thirty years by then, even being married to one of the major dog lovers of our time and living surrounded by a gazillion dogs, but Greta had my heart instantly. And she turned out to be one of the greatest dogs I ever had, and surely one of the dogs I loved most. She had just a wonderful loving nature, despite her funny looks. And one of her other sisters came to me a year later, when her owner died, Cookie. But Greta remained my most beloved dog. She lived to be thirteen, and had a terrific life with us. She became the queen of the house—after all, she was Mom's dog. So I became one of the dog lovers too.

My beloved dog Greta
(with the class-three malocclusion underbite)
Danielle Steel

But everyone knows that, just like people, not all dogs are perfect, and there have been a few lemons in our lives. Sweet Pea remains on the debatable list. And in the No Good Deed Goes Unpunished category, John's mother passed away two years after we were married. She had had a standard dachshund named Trixie who was fourteen years old, barked incessantly, and was unfriendly, but John insisted we take her, and he said, "How much longer can she live at fourteen?" I decided he was right and agreed. The answer to that question was: nearly forever. She lived to be twenty-one and spent seven years barking in my house.

And many years later, when I remarried, I gave my new husband the dog of his dreams: a Rhodesian ridgeback, a splendidly beautiful, graceful, but enormous creature. Ridgebacks are trained to chase lions in their native South Africa and run like the wind. But they are also one-man dogs, and this one had some sort of personality disorder, and like Sweet Pea, he did not like me, protective of his owner perhaps and possessive of him. The dog slept on our bed, and if I moved during the night, he emitted horrifying growls and bared his fangs at me. From a dog that weighed more than I did and was taller, these were not welcome signs of affection. I gave that dog a wide berth. And he once chased Victoria's Chihuahua, whom I rescued in the nick of time. I was very sad to see the

*Samantha with Mia and Vanessa with
Gidget, when both were puppies*
Danielle Steel family photo

marriage end several years later, but utterly thrilled to see the ridgeback leave. He was one scary dog, although he adored his master. He convinced me I was not a "big dog" person.

But on the whole, our experiences with dogs have been wonderful. And Greta had turned me into a dog lover again. Her eventual successor, Gracie, also a miniature Brussels griff, is just as sweet. It's a breed that suited me perfectly for a long time. They're lovely, easygoing, and sleep a lot, which works for me, since they sleep while I work. For twenty years, I couldn't see myself with any other breed. And although I thought my kids' dogs were very cute and had nice personalities, I couldn't imagine having a dachshund—they're too mischievous and bark a lot (which would drive me crazy while I write). Yorkies just didn't seem like "me" and were a little too cute. I couldn't even begin to imagine myself with a dog as small as a Chihuahua. My son's miniature Boston bull was way too active for me, since I write for eighteen and twenty hours at a time when I'm in the heat of a book or facing a tight deadline. My writing schedule can be very intense at times and requires concentration. So I was sure that Brussels griffs were the breed for me, until I moved back to Paris part-time, and commuted to California and New York every three or four weeks. And after seven years of commuting, I decided that I wanted a dog I could take with me, so I could have a dog in Paris too, and my Brussels griffs were too heavy for the weight limit to take in the cabin on the plane.

Suddenly I found myself looking longingly for a smaller dog to travel with me. I was lonely in Paris without one. But I couldn't figure out a breed I wanted that was small enough. It was like dating as I read dog books, cruised pet stores, and visited breeders, hoping to find a dog I'd fall in love with. The search was on.

Minnie as a tiny baby in the pet store
the day I found her
Victoria Traina

TWO

Looking for True Love (Again)

Once I decided I missed the warmth and companionship of a dog to take with me on my travels, and on the plane to Paris, I began a serious search. To me a dog provides someone to talk to, play with, take care of, and cuddle up with at night. Even if you have someone special in your life, a dog is a great companion. And watch out for men (or women) who don't like dogs. If you do love animals, someone who can't relate to yours may have an important piece missing that could matter to you. I've only had two men in my life who really disliked dogs, and I would have done better to avoid them both completely! I don't know many men who love dogs as much as my husband John—and with the arrangement he made, where I got the back end and he got the front end, he had a pretty sweet deal. But John always had room in his heart for a lot of kids and dogs!

I spent all my early years with pugs, and twenty adult years with Brussels griffs, and I just couldn't imagine another breed that would suit me. But pugs weigh about twenty pounds, shed a lot, and can be smelly, and griffs are fourteen or fifteen pounds, and there is no negotiating with the international airlines about their twelve-pound limit for a dog in the cabin, so I had to find a smaller dog. But none of the tiny breeds appealed to me. I looked at miniature Pomeranians (ugh—yappy!!), Yorkies, some of whom are really cute and some not so cute. Miniature dachsies, too barky though very sweet. Maltese were too active. Chihuahuas didn't appeal to me either, although two of my daughters have lovely ones, and they were the right size. And I looked at what I call the "poo" dogs, the currently fashionable/popular combos of cockapoo, yorkiepoo, maltipoo, and a whole bunch of other "poos" that seemed unpredictable to me as to how big they would be, and what traits they would have of either breed. And I didn't want a French poodle, which seemed too fussy to me, and they bark a lot too. And all I needed was a dog that would bark for twelve hours straight on a plane. Two of my daughters fly for work constantly and take their dogs with them, a miniature Yorkie and a teacup Chihuahua, but I still wasn't convinced.

I looked at a Havanese, kind of a fluffball from Cuba, and several Japanese breeds, but I didn't fall in love with them either. I even went completely off the deep end with a very unusual breed, a "hairless Chinese Crested," which looks like some kind of child's game where you put unrelated parts together. They have absolutely *no* fur, none, just skin with a lot of freckles, and at the end of their tail and on top of their head is a pouf of what looks like a bleached blond wig. It is the silliest-looking dog you've ever seen, and I loved the oddity of it, but it was so ugly that even I couldn't make myself take that leap, and it was going to be too big for the airline weight limit. I've written about a hairless Chinese Crested in a book, and really liked the breed because it was so incongruous. But the reality was a little too extreme. On top of it they frequently lose their teeth, and their tongues hang out! I often write dogs into my books, and have some real fun with it. It can add a wonderful element to a book.

A friend who went to a pet shop with me one day, in New York, was exasperated, and said "*What* are you looking for?" I said I didn't know, but whatever it was, I would know it when I saw it. I knew I had to fall in love with it, because otherwise all the work, time, energy, and love I'd have to invest in it just wouldn't be worth it. I tried to explain that to me, a dog, like a house or especially a person, has to be about "romance." The friend rolled his eyes at me. And by then I figured that I probably wouldn't get a dog to travel with me after all, since I had looked at dogs of every breed, and I was dogged (sorry!) about going to reliable pet stores and breeders I knew, and checking them out regularly for several months, but no dog had snagged my heart. Yet.

In early November, going through New York, on my way from Paris to California, I visited a pet store where I'd bought dogs before. I looked all the dogs over and saw nothing I fell in love with and was about to leave, when one of the salesmen I know well looked at me conspiratorially and said, "Wait." I stood there, wondering what he had in mind, nearly convinced that I'd be traveling alone forever, when he emerged with the tiniest dog imaginable in his arms. She was snow white, with enormous ears. She had ears and a face a bit like Yoda in *Star Wars,* big brown eyes, and a tiny milk-chocolate brown nose. She seemed very timid, but gazed straight at me. She weighed barely a pound, and fit in one of my hands (and I have very small hands, as I am a small person). He handed her to me, and she put her head on my shoulder and wrapped her mouse-sized paws around my neck. Bingo!!! It was love at first sight. She was a teacup Chihuahua, but small even for her breed. They said that she would weigh two or three pounds at most, full grown. She was eight weeks old. She was so tiny I was almost afraid to hold her—she looked more like a large mouse. Her ears were ridiculously oversize, and I kept reminding myself that I didn't want a dog that small. What if someone stepped on her? Even my daughters' Chihuahuas were hardier, this one was so tiny. I reasoned with myself as I stood there, telling myself that I needed something sturdier to travel with, that I never wanted a Chihuahua, that I would now officially become one of those weird old women with pink hair carrying a Chihuahua in a pink sweater. And as I told myself all the reasons why I didn't/shouldn't want her, I heard a voice say "I'll take her." Who said that? Omigod, I did! What had I just done? A Chihuahua? But you can't argue with love once it hits.

I had the same feeling I'd had about Greta all those years before, when she'd arrived uninvited from Ohio, with her funny face and class-three malocclusion underbite. I was in love, which was what I had said I wanted, regardless of breed. If I wanted to fall in love, this was it. And how could I fall in love with a dog? Don't ask me how, but I did. My daughter Victoria was with me, who encouraged me to get her, and at least two of my other daughters had warned me that I didn't need another dog and said it was a stupid idea. But stupid or not, I did it. Feeling dazed and a little giddy and actually guilty for being so self-indulgent, I handed them my credit card and bought her, as they told me she was too young to take with me, and I'd have to wait three or four more weeks to take her home.

Victoria, who was my partner in crime that day, offered to bring her when she came home for Thanksgiving, and I then proceeded to pick out pink water bowls, two beds, a bunch of collars that looked small enough for a hamster, and the smallest toys they had, which were bigger than she was. I was besotted, and my children's predictions were already coming true. I had owned her for five minutes, and I was already turning into one of those weird women I was terrified of becoming. I had become the owner of a tiny white long-haired teacup Chihuahua, and I had the frightening feeling that my life was about to change dramatically. And with the same kind of exultation mixed with terror you feel when you meet someone you are instantly crazy about, I went back to my hotel, knowing I had fallen in love with a one-pound dog. But who could resist those tiny mouse paws around my neck? For me, a puppy promises love and cozy moments, companionship and comfort, and that feeling that all is well in the world. In a way, it is a sign of hope.

It was late afternoon when I left the tiny white puppy at the pet shop, and I had dinner plans that night, and I came back to the pet shop alone that evening before dinner to hold her again. And as we saw each other and she snuggled in my arms, I knew I was hooked. She didn't even have a name yet. My daughter had suggested Yoda because she looked like him.

I was thinking of Blanche Neige, which is Snow White in French. And when I told a friend about her, he suggested Minnie Mouse, which seemed perfect for her. Minnie. I loved it, almost as much as I loved the tiny white Chihuahua.

Life suddenly seems so simple when you fall in love with a puppy. I smiled every time I thought of her. And no matter how crazy anyone thought I was to get her, I knew I had done the right thing. In an imperfect world full of heartbreak and disappointments, after looking high and low for her for several months, Minnie Mouse and I had found each other. It was exactly what I had hoped for when I started looking, it was true love. What more could I want?

Baby Minnie comes home

Alessandro Calderano

THREE

Minnie Comes Home

Knowing that Minnie wouldn't arrive in San Francisco for a few weeks, it took me a while to confess to what I'd done. Puppy? What puppy? Where? We had taken a few snapshots of her with a cell phone, and I started showing them to friends. She looked so sweet nestled in my hand. I told my children about her, some of whom declared me officially insane. They reminded me that I had dogs in San Francisco— what was I doing buying another dog? Fortunately, Victoria kept assuring me I'd done the right thing and remained enthusiastic, which kept me from having second thoughts. I tried explaining to the others that she would travel with me, which made sense to one or two of them.

But for the most part my kids shook their heads, and one earnestly said to me, "Now don't go all weird on us." But let's be realistic. In today's world having nine kids already makes me "different." How many people do that nowadays? And if being crazy about a puppy would make me officially eccentric, did I really care? Probably not. Why not? I find that as time goes by, Why not? is often the right answer. Why not do something you love? Why not take a chance and do something new, or stick your neck out, or even fall in love with a puppy? Who was I hurting by stretching my heart to include one more tiny being? Was that really so terrible? I think not.

Also, more than most of us like to admit, it's a lonely world, at every age. My kids have grown up and have their own very busy lives, and many of them have moved to other cities, and now so have I. I am only at home in San Francisco part-time, and even when I am, my kids in the same city are too busy to spend much time with me, which is as it should be. They have jobs, careers, spouses, boyfriends, girlfriends, lives. I don't expect them to sit around holding my hand. Once upon a time my house was filled with my kids, and their army of friends, and their many dogs. I was married and juggling an overfull life like a high-wire act, balancing a salami on my nose. Now my house is quiet, only one "child" lives at home, recently graduated from college, and she works all day and is out every night. And what kid in their twenties wants to hang around with their parents? None that I know. But that leaves the parents to fill their lives as best they can. It works better (I think, but who knows?) if you are married or have a partner to share your life with. If not, it makes for some very long quiet nights, compared to what it was when married with kids at home. As one friend says, "That was then, this is now," allegedly a Chinese proverb. And the last thing I want to do, personally, is hang on my children and expect them to fill the voids in my life. They have their own lives to live and destinies to follow, and I have mine. I had those same busy years in my twenties, discovering the world that they are entering now. I don't expect or even want them to drag me along like so much baggage. They need to be free to pursue their own paths. But then I have to follow my own, and change is not always easy when, for one reason or another, unexpectedly, you are alone.

In the game of life's musical chairs, you don't always get a chair, and then it's up to us to figure out how to fill our time and make it a good life. I'm very fortunate to have work that I really enjoy, good friends, and wonderful kids. But I find that no one who is still married or in partnership realizes or remembers how incredibly silent and lonely life can be when you're alone. Can a dog take the place of a person you love? No. A dog is not a person. But lacking a human to spend your time and life with, a dog can be a wonderful companion, warm your heart, and make you feel good about life. A dog can be an antidote to depression, a good excuse to get exercise, someone/something to take care of, to dedicate yourself to, even to worry about. A dog can make you smile, or just snuggle with you at night. They make the elderly feel loved and teach the young to be responsible. There are many, many good reasons to have a dog.

And loneliness is not unique to the elderly or even the middle-aged. I think solitude and loneliness are the new *mal du siècle* and affect every age. I see young people who are extremely lonely now. It's a tough subject, but suicide is more common now among the young than ever before. Something is missing in our lives. And some of the technological advancements (texting, e-mail) have made it fabulously easy to communicate, but they leave people without companionship and the everyday contact with other humans that has been an important constant in our lives, or even the sound of a human voice. (Most young people text each other, and don't call.)

More and more, young people are doing independent studies in college, which is probably more interesting than sitting through boring lectures, but it removes them from daily contact with other kids their age. Similarly, many jobs are done by computer from home now, or businesses are started from home to keep overhead low, which again means no daily contact with other people. And the sudden appearance in recent years of online dating services is a strong indicator that people are having a hard time meeting. Romances begin and end online, often with too little contact in between. Texting has almost replaced the phone, so suddenly you don't hear the voice of someone you care about. Young people actually end romances and "dump" each other by text. (What incredibly bad manners!!)

We have lost a lot of contact with other living beings. (And I know for myself that I get far more work done at home, without distractions, than I ever did in an office, but it is much more solitary, and you meet fewer people that way.) The world has changed. And many young people prefer urban colleges and universities to campuses in rural areas. And once in an urban setting, they are alone in studio apartments at eighteen or nineteen, leading the lives that used to be reserved for twenty-three- and twenty-five-year-olds after college. For a multitude of reasons, many people are isolated now, have less opportunity to meet new people of either sex, at every age. And they need companionship in that void. A dog won't change all of that, but it provides undeniable companionship, affection, and even humor in circumstances where people find themselves alone.

I know that my own children, previously in urban colleges, and now in the early years of their careers, have derived enormous comfort from their dogs. Our dogs become an important part of our lives, not to replace people, but as an added solace and support system that is not negligible. To non-dog-lovers, that affection for their dogs may be hard to understand, but I think it has strong emotional and psychological value, which cannot be denied. And studies have shown that the elderly derive great joy from dogs too. We all need love, it doesn't always come from the sources we hope for, but if it can be provided by a devoted, loving animal, what harm is there in that? For me, my loving puppy can really take the edge off a bad day, when she makes me smile or laugh.

So although many people, or even some of my kids, may not have understood why I'd want the inconvenience of a new dog, it made perfect sense to me. And yes, any other living being in your life can be an inconvenience. But love is inconvenient, life is inconvenient, even a canary is inconvenient. (You have to clean its cage.) But along with the chores and responsibilities comes the incredible blessing of loving and being loved. It sounds like a good trade-off to me. And as someone wise said, "Love is messy." What isn't? A puppy is messy. But I think the "messy" part is worth all the great stuff that comes with it. My kids were "messy" too, my marriages and the men I was married to, but I wouldn't trade a minute of the life I shared with them. But there is no doubt for me, the

My current Brussels griffon,
my favorite: Gracie
Cassio Alves

Ruby, one of my Brussels griffs
Cassio Alves

love of a dog is a great consolation prize now that the kids are gone!!

So I began preparing for Minnie's arrival. I felt considerable remorse toward my other dogs. Every time I left Gracie to go to Paris, she always looked so sad when she saw my valises come out, although I leave her with good people at my home to care for her. But I felt guilty not being able to take her or my other griffs with me. Try explaining to a faithful dog that she is three pounds over the weight limit for Air France! And introducing Minnie seemed like bringing a new baby home. She was going to be an interloper, an intruder, and being so young and tiny, she was going to get all the attention for a while. Ugh. I felt like a beast. Worse yet, this wasn't an ordinary-size puppy I could introduce to my other dogs. True confessions: I have four miniature Brussels griffs. Gracie is very much a lady, gentle to the core, and I knew she would cause no harm even to a one-pound puppy. One pound? I have shoes that are bigger and weigh more than that. A Big Mac is bigger than that. Which is also why I had never wanted such a tiny dog. I literally had nightmares, imagining her slipping into some tiny space on the airplane when we traveled, or getting stuck under my bed at home. She was soooo small!!!

And while I trusted Gracie with her, I didn't trust my other dogs. Ruby, the youngest, is bigger than Gracie and exuberant, and loves to swat things. One fast-moving paw, even in play, could have broken Minnie's back. It was definitely more like having a mouse than a dog! And my two other griffs, Meg and Hope, were older and crankier and were not likely to take kindly to her, and I was not willing to take that risk. So Minnie would have to be separate from the other dogs, which took some planning and organizing as to who would be where when. Minnie had to be protected from the other dogs.

I was also worried about people stepping on her, and the solution I came up with was a baby playpen to keep her in, to keep her safe. Now she is full grown at two pounds, and she runs around freely, but whenever I want to keep her safe if there are too many people around (like a Sunday-night casual dinner party in my Paris kitchen), I put her in the playpen, and she's happy there. The vet had also warned me that I couldn't sleep with her—I could roll over on her and kill her, or she could fall off the bed—so I still put her in the playpen to sleep at night. It is a perfect place to keep her safe. I cuddle with her before I go to sleep, but then I place her in her bed in the playpen. I wish I could put her in bed with me, she's so cozy, but I just can't. (Gracie spends the night on my bed, and sometimes Ruby too, hopping on and off occasionally.) A dog as tiny as Minnie is a big responsibility.

*Hope, one of my current
Brussels griffs*

Cassio Alves

*Meg, also one of my current
Brussels griffs*

Cassio Alves

I got the puppy food she needed, the bowls I'd picked out in New York arrived, the igloo beds, and Wee-Wee Pads to train her where to go (she learned on the first day and makes no mistakes). I had collars and leashes, and a few toys. I bought all kinds of squeaky toys, tiny sweaters, little pink blankets (okay, I'll confess: a tiny wool hat with holes for her ears, which she hates and won't wear), and I got ready to spoil her totally. So sue me, I was excited that she was coming home. There are worse indulgences than spoiling a dog. It's not a crime, and I had so much fun getting ready for her.

As promised, my daughter Victoria took her home in New York, a week before they came home for Thanksgiving, so Minnie got a taste of being loved and spoiled before she got to me. And Victoria also has a Chihuahua, Tallulah, who I don't think was too pleased by Minnie's visit.

And then the big day arrived, the day before Thanksgiving, my kids came home and two of my daughters flew home with Minnie. They said she had slept the whole way on the trip. We took her out of her carrying bag and introduced her to her new world, my bedroom, the playpen, and at first the only place she was happy was the playpen. She was terrified when I put her on my bedroom carpet, and she only ventured a few inches from the playpen and was happy whenever we put her back into her safe, contained little world. Everything must have looked huge to her. Now she runs around my room, my office, the Paris apartment, and everywhere else like a maniac. Now this is her domain. But at first she was scared to death, and it took her some days to adjust to it.

She went to the vet to get checked out and was fine. We got travel papers for her, and everyone who saw her was amazed by how tiny she was. And I hated it when anyone picked her up—I was afraid they'd drop her or she'd get hurt, she was just so small. (I stepped on her paw once myself and panicked over it, but she was fine.) She was definitely a happy addition to our world. And she was an incredible gift for me, someone to fuss over, take care of, and nurture, after so many years of so many kids and dogs.

With a sigh of happiness, I settled into caring for her. And when the kids left on the Sunday night after Thanksgiving, it was a little less agonizing than usual. I had Minnie, and we were leaving for New York and Paris the next day. I packed more stuff than for a baby, for our two days in New York, and for her new life in Paris. Minnie had no idea what was in store for her, the day I put her in her black sweater and collar, and placed her gently in her carrying bag. Minnie was about to become a world traveler! And I felt like I was carrying precious cargo as I picked up her bag. And for once, other than worrying about if I had a book I liked or if I had enough work in my briefcase to keep me busy, or if the movies on the plane would be decent, I had Minnie to think about instead of myself. It was exactly what I had wanted when I set out to find her. And as we left on a red-eye flight that night, it felt like she had always been part of my life.

Minnie in her travel bag

Alessandro Calderano

FOUR

Minnie Goes to Paris

In order to travel domestically and internationally with a dog, you have to have health papers showing her vaccinations and ID papers. She has to be under the weight limit (twenty pounds domestically and twelve pounds internationally) and be confined in a carrier to go in the cabin with you. You have to purchase a dog ticket for her, $125 domestically and $200 internationally. A dog over the weight limit can go in the cargo section in a crate, but there are risks involved, and some dogs don't survive the trip. It's too hot or too cold, depending on the time of year, or they're just too traumatized by the experience. I have never been willing to take the risk of putting an animal in cargo. And of course we went through all the requirements of taking her in the cabin, since she is only two pounds.

She had to be in a dog carrier for the flight. And you are not allowed to take the dog out of his or her travel bag. There are a huge variety of carriers in a multitude of shapes, styles, and sizes, depending on the size of the dog and the taste of the owner. Like all hand luggage, there are limits to how big it can be, just like the weight of the dog, but as long as the bag meets the cabin requirements, after that it's a free-for-all. You can get carriers in every color, everything from camouflage to plaid to pink with rhinestones on it. The most important feature to me was that Minnie could see out of the bag. The dog carriers I had had in the distant past had netting on all four sides, so the dog could look around freely. I went shopping for something a little more fun and stylish and better suited to Minnie and her new wardrobe (the old bag I had was a fairly ugly black nylon), only to discover that netting on all four sides had gone out of style, I'm not sure why. I found only one with netting she could see through on three sides, and most of them had netting only on either end, like little windows, which seemed very dark and confining to me. Given the long hours she was going to spend in the bag, I didn't want her to feel like she was in a shoe box. The bags I looked at seemed seriously claustrophobic to me.

I even went to two famous French handbag and luggage shops, who were proud of their dog carriers, and although they were very stylish, in some really jazzy colors (orange, red, royal blue), they were narrow, with a tiny little window at each end, and I decided you really had to hate your dog and be seriously narcissistic to choose fashion over the comfort of the dog and show off with one of those fancy bags. I wound up traveling with our old bag, with four sides she could see out of (and I could see her) and a convenient pocket to put her supplies in, and I have continued to use it. It is definitely not chic, but she seems happy in it, and she can check out what's going on around her. I suppose one theory is that maybe a dog would feel cozy in a small dark bag, but those bags sure didn't appeal to me. Mine has zippers at both ends and another one on top, and it's roomy enough for her. I like it a whole lot better than any new bag I saw—especially the fancy ones, which cost a fortune and also weigh a ton. My old one is much lighter. And I think it's worth looking around for a bag your dog will be happy in, not just one you think looks stylish. You can find relatively new carriers at secondhand stores. I recently gave away the ones I don't use, and others do the same. And the old ones might suit you and your dog a lot better.

As soon as we got to the airport, someone from the airline (who has to see the dog—they think maybe I'm carrying a skunk instead of a dog?) asked if she was a service dog. I was stumped by the question. I've never heard of a one-pound Chihuahua being used as a seeing-eye dog. And the only other kind of service dog I know about is for epileptics. Apparently dogs can be trained to sense signs of a seizure before the person with the seizure is aware of it, and can warn them, which is very impressive. But other than that, I knew of no service dogs. And I looked blank when the woman from the airline asked the question. Service dog? (I actually used that in a book, when a man with one arm was taking Stanley, his huge bloodhound, on the flight with him, and when questioned, he ironically said the dog cuts his meat, and they let him fly in the cabin.) I could think of no way for Minnie to be a service dog, and I asked the woman to explain what she meant, which she did, much to my amazement.

She said that if Minnie was just a pet or companion dog, she had to have all the paperwork. For entry into Europe, she also needed an international chip, which she had (not just an American one—it's about the size of a grain of rice under their skin, but when scanned, it gives all the owner's ID information. Modern technology!). And she needed a ticket, which we also had. *But* if I told the airline that I was too afraid to fly without my dog, in that case I could take a dog of *any* size onto the plane with me (even a Great Dane or a Saint Bernard), it does not need to be contained, it can lie openly and unconfined at my feet, needs no paperwork, and flies for free, with no ticket! I was stunned. All you need, if you declare her as a service dog, is a letter from your doctor confirming that you're afraid to fly and need your dog freely with you and not confined. I was amazed. So there was poor Minnie, flying like a prisoner in a carrying bag, but if she had been a service dog, she could have sat on my lap for the entire flight. It didn't seem fair to me, particularly given how small she was, but those were the rules. So I learned something new that night!

The trip to New York went smoothly. Minnie slept for most of it. I even got up the nerve to sneak Minnie out of her bag, since it was dark in the cabin, and she slept on my chest, under a blanket for a while. I loved it, and so did she! My daughters who travel with their dogs had sternly warned me never to take her out of her bag on a flight, or I'd spoil her. What can I tell you? I'm a spoiler. Minnie is well behaved anyway, never cries or barks in her travel bag, and is a perfect traveler. She sleeps during the entire trip, and if I peek in the bag to check on her, she looks at me sleepily as though to say, "What? What do you want?" (She likes her travel bag so much that sometimes she climbs into it at home and goes to sleep. It's cozy for her.)

We got to the hotel in New York. My daughter had dropped off the playpen she had used at her apartment for Minnie, and

I had brought a small bed for her in the suitcase. Minnie settled right in, and our stay in New York went fine. I had everything with me that she needed. And it was way too cold in New York in November to take her out. So the first and only problem I encountered was dressing her two days later to leave for Paris. I had bought several sweaters for her, and she had hand-me-downs from my daughters' Chihuahuas, and I had also bought a little padded quilted coat, kind of like a snowsuit for really cold weather. My daughters had informed me that in freezing-cold weather, she needed to wear a sweater *and* the coat. I've never had a dog that small, and they are fragile in the cold. I dressed nine babies for the cold and even took them skiing, so I wasn't going to be daunted by dressing a one-pound baby Chihuahua. I was a pro.

As it turned out, babies are easier to dress in winter clothes than baby Chihuahuas. I packed up all of Minnie's gear to leave for the airport. I put a blanket in her carrying bag, a Wee-Wee Pad, and a couple of toys. I had food for the trip and two bowls, one each for food and water. I even carried a spare sweater and Baby Wipes in my purse. I got dressed and put the sweater and coat on Minnie and stood her up in the playpen (she was not looking too happy about her outfit). I turned around to put on my coat.

Then I turned around again to pick her up and put her in

Minnie in Paris for the first time
Alessandro Calderano

Minnie in the Paris apartment kitchen
Alessandro Calderano

the carrying bag—and found Minnie lying on her back with her four legs straight up in the air. Oops. For a minute I thought she was sick, and then realized she had just rolled over. I stood her back up on her feet and watched her roll over and stick her feet up in the air again, like a beetle on its back. By then I noticed that she was glaring at me, and she made it clear. If I was going to put her in those miserable clothes, she was not going to stand up. Every time I stood her up, she rolled over on her back again. The wardrobe issue was not going well. (For a minute, I was reminded of my son Nick at three, when I put him in an adorable one-piece suit with a giraffe on it. He looked at it in horror and said, "You expect me to wear *that?*" Minnie appeared to feel the same way about her snowsuit, although it was very cute.) And I couldn't take it off because I didn't want her to freeze when we left the hotel, and it was bitter cold. I intended to take it off on the plane and not before.

I put her in the bag, and she was quiet on the way to the airport. I didn't peek into the bag and assumed she was okay. And finally at the airport, I took a look, and she was lying flat on her face. Oops again. Another wardrobe crisis. I took a closer look and realized she had slipped both front paws *into* the snowsuit and was balancing on her nose. That's what I mean about dogs making you laugh. She looked so funny, I had to chuckle. And we were clearly going to have some issues about her clothes. I took her snowsuit off on the plane and left her sweater on, and she looked relieved.

And once on the Air France flight, I got a taste of the differences between domestic travel and being on a French plane. The French are crazy about dogs. Americans love their dogs too, but they are much more rigid about regulations. On the flight from San Francisco to New York, I had been sternly warned by the most unfriendly flight attendant not to take her out of the bag under any circumstances. They never asked what was in it, if it was a puppy, and were not interested. Rules were rules. On the Air France flight, every single member of the crew who walked past us wanted to know what it was, could they see her, and asked me to open the bag, and then oohed and ahhed over her, wanted to pet her, and a couple of them winked at me and indicated that if I took her out during the flight, they would turn a blind eye, and did I want any treats for her? (No, I didn't, since she was on a puppy diet.) But it was sweet how friendly they were. And they still are on every Air France flight we take. It's the same in French restaurants. If you bring a dog, it is normal to set a place at the table for your dog and serve it a meal, which horrifies Americans. French dogs are treated like people!

Minnie slept on the flight, and when we got to the apartment in Paris, she discovered her second home. I had a play-pen waiting for her there, and some supplies. I unpacked her toys, her beds, her blankets, and her bowls. (I'd brought her American puppy food so she didn't have to change diet. I tried to think of everything.) She scampered around the kitchen and made herself at home. And my housekeeper fell in love with her on the spot. She was so unbelievably cute, and so happy to find her toys when she got there.

And in Paris, she barked for the first time. She had occasionally made tiny squeaking mouse noises but so far had never barked. I discovered rapidly that she hated the fax machine when a fax came in (and the ice maker). Otherwise, she rarely barks. She is as untechnological as I am. I try to restrain myself and generally don't bark at the fax machine, although I'd like to when my office or attorneys send me thirty-page faxes. Minnie does the barking for me. The fax machine makes her irate. She's happy and good-natured the rest of the time.

Minnie's life in Paris is busier, or different, than her life in the States. In New York we stay in a hotel. In San Francisco, where my office is, if I have a busy day, she hangs out in the office in the daytime, and thinks everyone is there to keep her company, and then she comes back to me at the end of the day. That way I don't have to leave her alone. And in Paris, I have a huge kitchen, which is centrally located, so I put her there in the daytime, and every time someone comes through the kitchen, she is delighted to see them. Wherever she is, she is thrilled to see people, and they are happy to see her. Everyone exclaims at her tiny size, and she has gotten brave and gregarious, loves to play, and runs all over the place. She seems to be convinced that whoever comes in is there to entertain and visit her. Although in the beginning she was very shy, she no longer is. She loves company!

She has favorite places to hang out, a warm spot on the floor where the heating passes through. I put a small bed for her there, a pink bed next to my desk where my computer is (which I only use for e-mail, not for writing), and I found an adorable red "house," which is also a bed, that I use to store her toys. She loves the bed on the "hot" spot, and the one next to my desk. When I'm sending e-mails, she comes and lies in it, to be close to me. And her various options keep her busy.

First, she rummages in her heap of toys on the floor and puts several in one of her beds. Then she gets into the bed, plays with the toys for a while, and decides she wants some of them somewhere else. So one by one, she takes them to a different bed, piles them up, gets in, plays again, and then moves some of them to one of the other options. I don't know what she's thinking, but there is clearly a method to her madness.

Minnie with her toys

Alessandro Calderano

Minnie in her bed next to the "hot spot" on the floor
(next to a dog statue she ignores)

Alessandro Calderano

She reorganizes her toys several times a day. And she has favorites among her toys. I carry those in my hand luggage so they don't get lost. (I know, it sounds silly, but old habits die hard.) And her *very* favorite toy is a little gray mouse she loves to play with and puts in her bed!

The game of "fetch" makes no sense to Minnie. You throw her a toy, she grabs it, tosses it around, and starts to run back to you with it, and then you can see her think better of it, change her mind at the last minute, figure she's not going to give you a toy she loves, and run away and hide it. She can play with her toys for hours. And she seems to be convinced that we are all trying to steal them, and she is not going to let that happen.

Similarly, she is convinced we are going to eat her kibble. Several times a day she fills her mouth with as many grains of kibble as she can stuff in it, and then goes somewhere to hide it. You can see plainly where the kibble is, although sometimes she'll hide it under her bed. If she sees you watching her do it, she'll hide it again. And then she gives us a suspicious look. Recently, she piled it on top of her igloo bed, saw that I had noticed it, and then went to get a doll and put it on top of the kibble to hide it better. To date, her suspicions are unfounded, and I have not eaten her kibble yet. But she still suspects I might. It really makes me laugh when I watch her antics. She keeps busy for hours, and then collapses and goes to sleep. She is an endless source of amusement and joy. And it's a lot more fun watching her than stressing over a rewrite or a slew of faxes to answer or any of life's less fun events. It's hard to be sad with a funny little being bouncing around, doing things that make you laugh. She is definitely the best therapy there is, which is why dogs make people so happy. Whoever comes to visit winds up laughing at her, and everyone in the house is in love with her. She is impossible to resist. And in Paris I can spend more time lying on the floor playing with her.

Her Paris wardrobe is also a lot jazzier than her clothes for San Francisco. (I dress better in Paris too and wear mostly jeans in San Francisco, because I go out more in Paris, so I get more dressed up.) I've discovered a few stores, and one in particular, that have incredibly silly but fun outfits for tiny dogs. Little sparkly sweaters, others with rhinestones on them, or heart designs, a pink snowsuit with a bunny on it (which she hates as much as the old one, this one even more so because it has a little hood). It is hysterically fun to dress her up, although she looks pained about it, an ordeal she must endure. The things I've found for her in Paris are so cute, although they potentially put me back in the "weird" category that my children warned me about and that I intended to avoid. I've

Paris fashion: Minnie in style
in her gray sweater with pink flower
Alessandro Calderano

given up—she looks adorable in her cute sweaters and coats, even a gray sweater with a pink flower on it. And she has equally fancy leashes in pink, white, red, and black patent leather, with flowers on them, or rhinestones. I can't help it, I have a ball dressing her up, and she's not a bull mastiff, after all, she's a two-pound teacup Chihuahua. One of my Paris friends said I should have called her Barbie Mouse since I love dressing her up. I recently got her a red wool coat with a black velvet collar that looks exactly like a coat my children had for Christmas when they were small.

There is also family history for dressing dogs. My kids loved Halloween and always planned their costumes for months. And they loved dressing their dogs in Halloween costumes too. One of them dressed their dog as a tiny bumblebee. Vanessa dressed her Yorkie one year as a French Maid. There were several "ballerinas" in tiny tutus. I think the prize of all time went to my son Maxx when he dressed Annabelle, his Boston bull, as Superwoman, in a Superman costume, cape and all, with a blond wig. Most pet stores carry costumes for dogs at Halloween, and they have bunny ears at Easter. I got Minnie tiny reindeer antlers for her first Christmas, but she hated them, so I didn't make her wear them. And my daughter Sam recently gave Minnie a bumblebee costume and tiny witch hat and orange coat for Halloween!

A little off the subject, but I have to mention that the super grand costume prize went to Beatrix's boyfriend, who made a costume that looked like her dog Jack, and he walked around the house dropping plastic "fleas" everywhere.

And others must fall prey equally to that indulgence of fashion for their dogs, since I saw a Great Dane in New York in a Burberry coat and an Hermès scarf. I know I could be doing something more intelligent with my time (and money), but I'm having fun. What's the harm in that, especially if it makes me happy?

And not only am I happy, but so is Minnie. You can tell that she knows she is much loved. She is constantly ready to play and in good humor. She never looks sad or unhappy. She has a very good life and seems to enjoy every minute of it, with comfortable beds, a heap of toys, regular food, kind visitors (who sometimes bring her new toys), and an adoring owner. It's an enviable life. And we improve each other's lives. She could have wound up in a less loving home, and I could still be alone during the months I spend in Paris. And even though my griffs are loving dogs, they aren't as playful or as affectionate as Minnie. We seem to be a perfect fit. And I do think there are good matches between owners and dogs. Some matches are not as easy and don't work out as well. Dogs who need more attention than their owners have time to give become lonely and depressed or resentful (like people). Some dogs live in homes where kids, or someone, mistreats them, which is unfortunate. Other dogs have been too badly abused previously to attach or even adjust. It takes wisdom, self-awareness, and a little bit of luck to make the right match.

And sadly, some dogs are just dogs. You can get a puppy who looks cute but grows up to have no personality and just turns out to be "a dog," rather than someone special. I've had one dog like that, and one of my daughters had one too. A close friend had a dog that grew up to be very dull. It was named Alice. Some dogs just turn out to be Alice, the way some people turn out to be bores. Not everyone has a great personality, and not all dogs do either. It's kind of disappointing when you discover you have one of those. It helps if they look like they have a sweet personality when you pick them. With people and animals, I am more seduced by personality than by looks. (As one friend said about the men she dated, she had a terrible weakness for beautiful, not-too-bright men. As she put it, when she finally moved on to more interesting, less handsome men, "Looks fade, but stupid is forever." It seems to apply to dogs too.)

We've all heard it said that dogs resemble their owners, and I always wonder if that's true. Minnie is amazingly good-natured, a little timorous and cautious at times. She likes to play, she hates the fax machine, and she likes to wear cute clothes. (She's gotten used to some of her outfits, or at least she tolerates them for me. We've compromised on some sweaters she doesn't mind, in bright colors—purple, pink, red, orange.) So maybe we're more alike than I realize. We both have delicate stomachs. But on the other hand, I don't hide my kibble. At least not yet. I could do a lot worse than being compared to Minnie.

One slightly odd thing happened the first time Minnie went to her Paris vet. I noticed afterward on the form that in describing her, he had written down that she was a white and tan Chihuahua, which wasn't accurate. She was snow white when I got her and when we arrived in Paris, so much so that while looking for a name for her, I had almost called her "Blanche Neige," as I mentioned earlier. "Minnie Mouse" seemed cuter and suited her better. But she was certainly not white and tan. I figured that the vet was just distracted and made a mistake, which didn't seem serious to me, so I didn't bother to call back and correct it.

A week or so later, as she played in the kitchen, I noticed a small smudge on her back, the size of a thumbprint. She is so constantly being loved and cuddled that I thought maybe someone with dirty hands had picked her up when I wasn't watching. I meant to wash off the spot but was busy and forgot about it. A few days after that I noticed a second tiny smudge. Who was picking up Minnie with dirty hands when I wasn't around? I washed the spots, and they didn't come off, which was even more annoying—what did that person have on their hands when they picked her up?

And the next day I was really upset. There was a fine dusting of pale, pale beige spots on one hip—someone had obviously spilled café au lait on her (coffee with *lots* of milk, which the French often drink for breakfast). Who could be that careless around Minnie? I hoped the coffee hadn't been hot when they spilled it, but she seemed perfectly happy. (And let's face it, like kids, dogs never care how dirty they are. A little dirt never hurt anyone!) But it still bothered me that she was being handled with dirty hands, and now someone was spilling coffee with milk on her. I mentioned it to my assistant, who loves her and she loves him, and he had noticed the spots too. But since Minnie was hanging out in the kitchen, having something spill on her could happen. We were puzzled.

But the day after, the café au lait spots were darker, and there were more of them, and over the next few weeks, suddenly Miss Minnie had acquired a whole bunch of small beige spots, dusted across her side and part of her back. They still looked like pale coffee spots, but now we knew that they weren't fingerprints or coffee drops, she actually had pale beige spots. They seemed funny looking at first, but now we're used to them. (I was highly insulted when a friend said jokingly, "You should have called her 'Spot.'") Over a period of several weeks, the spots came out and darkened a little, and they are indeed a kind of pale beige/tan color. She is still mostly white, but she does have these spots. The next time I saw the vet, he told me that white Chihuahuas almost always get those pale beige spots somewhere on their body, not all over, although they are invisible for the first few months. It explained his description of her as "white and tan." And to his discerning experienced eye, he had seen the first hint of them long before I did. So Minnie does have a dusting of pale beige spots and is no longer pure white. She is just as cute, they are almost rose-colored in places and very pale. But it's a good thing I didn't name her Snow White, or I might have had to add "with spots." Needless to say, I love her just as much with spots!

Thus far Minnie's international life only includes Paris. Theoretically, to go there she needs detailed paperwork that we have to apply for in advance *every* time she travels and leaves the country. It's a nuisance to redo it each time, but it can't be avoided. Customs officials are supposed to look at her travel documents and health certificates when she enters France, and returns to the United States, and I carry them diligently. But so far no one has ever looked at them in France, they just wave her through, and occasionally they look at her documents when we re-enter the States. But you always need the papers in case they want to see them.

The only problem I have had, and not a big one, has been with airport security in the United States. Each time they tell me to "strip" her, take off her collar, harness, leash, and all her clothes for a security check so they can "frisk" her. It always annoys me. Frightening-looking men saunter through security, and meanwhile they are frisking my trembling Chihuahua, who is terrified of them. And they actually do frisk her. Please. One of the security guards actually asked if she would "attack" them. Are you kidding? Being afraid of Minnie is like being afraid of a hamster—and in fact, the hamsters we had years ago were a lot fiercer than Minnie. But you have to follow the rules, and do as they ask, even if they want to frisk her.

If you travel, do *not* put your dog through the X-ray machine in its carrier on the moving belt! You don't have to, and it would frighten your dog unnecessarily. You can carry a small dog through in your arms, and then "strip" her when they ask you to. (Her leash and collar or harness—safer for tiny dogs with delicate necks—set off the metal detector.)

Britain has always been more rigid about bringing dogs into the country. For years, they had a quarantine, requiring you to leave your dog in a government kennel for six months, which kept most people from taking their dogs to England, unless they were moving there. (Elizabeth Taylor once chartered a boat to stay off-dock on the Thames, so she could bring her dogs into the country and not go through immigration or subject them to quarantine.) Recently, they lifted the quarantine but now require an aggressive worming process within twenty-four hours of entering the U.K., and a vet's certificate saying the worming process was performed.

I recently passed up what sounded like a fun weekend in London with friends because I didn't want to leave Minnie in Paris with other people, and when I checked out the worming for such a tiny dog, it was likely to make her sick for the whole duration of my stay in London. I didn't want to put her through it, and make her sick for no reason, so I passed on the trip, and we had a nice weekend in Paris instead.

So England is not on Minnie's travel map. Although the British love their dogs, they make it just too difficult to enter the country with one. I wasn't going to make Minnie sick for my London weekend! So sometimes having a puppy or a dog can hamper your mobility, even for a weekend with friends close to where you live. I still think it's worth it. And we've tackled no other foreign countries with her so far, just France, which is very easy, since the French are so hospitable to dogs.

Minnie in her "bumblebee" costume
Samantha Traina

There are of course other alternatives to traveling with your dog, if you don't want to take your dog with you, or feel you can't. You can leave them at a dog sitter's, or with a friend, although friendships have ended over dogs getting hurt or lost while in a friend's care. And nowadays there are some amazing boarding facilities for dogs. Several of my daughters travel a lot for business and occasionally have to board their dogs when they leave town (or leave them with each other if possible). And there is a whole new market for "dog hotels" in big cities, for young working people who can afford them. (There have always been caring reliable kennels that board dogs. And some you want to be careful of.) But the new breed of dog-boarding facility is mind-boggling.

For "regulars," they get a badge (like airline personnel) with their photo ID on them. And the owner gets to choose from a dizzying array of options. They ask you if you want your dog to have "group play," or be exercised, and played with alone. Do you want outdoor walks for them or keep them inside the facility? Do they have "friends" or "relatives" staying at the dog hotel you would like them to play with, and if so how many times a day? Dog bones, chew toys, special diet, grooming? It's like dropping a kid off at camp. And I know that when my "grand dogs" stay there, they room together, play together, are allowed to sit in the window for a certain amount of time, eat the menu my daughters choose for them, and get their hair done before they come home. Frankly, it sounds like a vacation I think I'd enjoy, and the dogs come home happy and looking very pleased with themselves. I'm afraid Minnie will never know the luxury of camp for dogs, since she travels with me. But it's also a comfort to my daughters to know their dogs are happy when they're away.

I am lucky enough to travel with Minnie, who is definitely an international dog. We speak to her in French, Italian, and English at home, and she responds to all three. Clearly, not only is Minnie well dressed, she is a genius! What a perfect dog!!

Minnie
Victoria Traina

FIVE

Having a Good Vet
(or: Sometimes Mother Knows Best!)

One thing that makes life simpler, if you have a dog, is having a good vet. I seem to apply a lot of the same principles to my dogs that I did to my kids. That probably sounds odd, but as I said, I am a "kid person" above all, even more than a dog person, and most of my life experience is with kids. That's probably better than if I were applying dog principles to my kids, although maybe that works too, as long as you're responsible and love your kids and dogs.

Before I took Minnie to Paris, I asked a friend in Paris for the name of a good vet. And she gave me the name of not a good vet but a great vet, with his own veterinary hospital, which is open 24/7. You don't want to be searching desperately for a vet or a pet hospital in the middle of the night if your dog has an accident or is seriously sick.

On the other hand, in Paris there is something called SOS Médecins (SOS Doctors) for when you feel too lousy to go out, aren't sick enough for the emergency room, but need medical help. They come to your house and are a very useful service. And they have the same thing with vets. But I feel better going to a vet I know and who knows my dog.

And the vet my friend recommended is fabulous. Not only medically, but he is kind, warm, terrific with my dog, and has a sense of humor, which always helps. He is a really nice person. In San Francisco we go to a very competent pet hospital two blocks from my house, which is great to have so nearby, but they have many vets, and I rarely see the same vet twice. So while their medical care is top notch, the personal touch is missing, and the vet on duty may not know my dog. In Paris, going to the same doctor who knows me and my dog is an added bonus.

The first time I took Minnie to her Paris vet, she had been making funny snorting sounds. As I said earlier, I've never had a dog with a proper nose. My pugs as a child, and my griffs as an adult, all have squashed noses. Minnie is my first dog with a real nose. And she took to snorting (which I think is due to the steam heat in the apartment). I was sure she was fine, but I wanted to be reassured that the snorting sounds were normal and not something like asthma. I diligently described to the doctor what she'd been doing. It was the first time we'd met. And much to my amusement, he imitated what I'd described, asking if that was the sound. It didn't seem like the right sound, so he asked if a second noise he demonstrated was the one. That didn't sound like it either, so he offered a third option, each time acting out the sound. And by then I had forgotten the first sound. I thought it was snort number three, but wanted to hear snort number one again. Straight faced, he went through the repertoire again, and after he did that several times, I decided that snort number three was it, which he said was called "reverse sneezing," which apparently Chihuahuas do, and some other breeds as well. Forevermore I will always think of him demonstrating the three snorts, without batting an eye. We became friends after that.

I was particularly glad that I had established a relationship with a vet, when one night I happened to notice that Minnie had found a pipe in my kitchen that I'd never noticed before. It was a few inches above the ground, and it was severely rusty. She was licking it when I saw her and shooed her away, but I was worried that either the rust flakes on the pipe or maybe even the paint might make her sick. She seemed fine but two hours later was vomiting violently, and I was panicked. It was three in the morning by then, and I had no idea if she'd been poisoned, or if she was just sick. But she's so tiny that seeing her so sick was terrifying. I called the all-night number at the vet, and the relief vet on duty told me to come in. I bundled Minnie up, and she looked miserable. I called a cab (who took forty minutes to come!) and asked a friend to come with me to the vet. I didn't want to be riding around alone in a cab at four a.m. with a desperately sick dog. They had already called poison control when we got there and thought it was unlikely that she'd been poisoned by the rusty pipe, although it was a possibility. They gave her a shot to stop the vomiting, we stayed there until six a.m., with impressively competent care, and they sent us home with two kinds of medicine to take for three days. Giving her the medicine with a dropper was an acrobatic (for me) adventure in itself. I was exhausted for the rest of the day, and Minnie was right as rain and hungry by noon. We later figured out that she'd eaten a piece of a toy, had gotten rid of it while vomiting, and was fine. But it was a huge relief to have a good vet to go to, who was instantly available.

We went back to see the regular vet the next day, and he put her on a special diet, which she loved. And the one time she got an upset stomach in New York, I called him too. Now I consult him about my other dogs as well. It sounds crazy, but having a great vet is like having a great pediatrician for your kids. It's a must, and if you don't want to go to a high-end private vet, there are clinics for dogs too. And there's no question, having a dog with health problems can be expensive.

I think, as with anything in life, you need to trust your instincts. The vet knows medicine better than you do, particularly for complicated issues. But you know your dog better than anyone. Speak up, if you're not comfortable with the recommended treatment, or if their assessment seems wrong to you. Find a vet who will listen to you. Your knowledge of your dog will serve you well. Elmer, my basset hound, appeared to be dying of a mysterious disease and was fading away in front of me. Out of sheer desperation, and not knowing what else to do to make him comfortable, I took off his flea collar. He sprang back to life within hours. He had a near fatal allergy to the chemicals in the flea collar. (I made him a necklace of eucalyptus pods after that, which kept the fleas away. Sometimes more natural solutions work best.)

But if you feel your vet is overmedicating your dog, say so. I always prefer more conservative solutions to radical ones. It's sad to say, but vet hospitals are a profitable business and can sometimes be overzealous about prescribing medications, or even minor surgeries.

Minnie's only major medical procedure to date was getting

spayed. She looked traumatized by the experience and acted crabby and weird on the pain meds afterward, growling and barking at everyone, when she normally never barks. And she had to wear a plastic collar she hated. When the collar came off and we stopped the pain medication, she went back to her sweet self. I think she felt weird on the pain meds, which can happen to humans too.

And there is no question, medical procedures for dogs, and surgeries, can be shockingly expensive.

One of my friends has a dog with cancer, and the surgeries for him have been exorbitant. But if you can afford it, you do. We love our pets, and it can be a costly venture. There is medical insurance for dogs now, which may be worth looking into.

When my friend discovered that her dog has cancer, I was devastated for her and tried to think what I could do. There wasn't much I could do, other than offer comfort and sympathy, and then I thought of something, which meant a great deal to her. I hired a dog photographer to take beautiful photographs of her dog, so that one day she would have all those pictures to remember him by. Fortunately, the dog is doing well, but she is very happy to have the album of photos. And I'm sure she will treasure them one day. It's a nice thing to be able to do for a friend at a hard time.

Losing an animal we love is so painful. And we've been through that too, particularly as my children started to lose their childhood dogs recently. With much sadness, we just lost the last one. We remember them fondly, with great love for all the years we shared with them. We have a little pet cemetery in our backyard in California, with the rabbits the kids had as children, and our beloved dogs. The dog of the original owner of the house, Sugar, is still there too. We have little stone headstones to honor each of them.

One of the many things I am happy about with Minnie is that Chihuahuas usually live for a long time, some for close to twenty years. Longevity is something to keep in mind when you buy a dog, although I would have bought Minnie no matter what breed she was. When you fall in love, you fall in love.

Maxx's Nancy: keeping busy in the office

Cassio Alves

SIX

The Gift that Keeps on Giving

More than once I have done something that no sane person should ever try to do: give someone I love a dog. It is an incredibly brave, and usually foolhardy, thing to do. And I have no idea why, but it has turned out well every time. It's a very gutsy thing to do. One thing you should try to be sure of is that the recipient *really* wants a dog! (The antique dealer who sent me Greta had no idea if I wanted one, but that turned out happily too.)

When my kids were little, I gave them their dogs as gifts and surprised them. They had been asking for a dog for a while, and the gift was always met with squeals of delight. My oldest daughter picked her dog, and I surprised her with her second one, which was never really an exciting dog, so I guess that wasn't a resounding success. Maxx's first Boston bull, Annabelle, was a surprise, which gave him endless joy for fourteen years. All three of Vanessa's Yorkies were surprises, and all three were major hits. Victoria picked out both of her Chihuahuas, and Sam her miniature dachshund, and all were beloved dogs, and Victoria's Chihuahua Tallulah still is.

But the really courageous and insane act has been giving dogs to friends, and each was a special case. The difficult thing with giving a dog to a friend is that sometimes people say they want something they really don't. Or they think they do, but the reality is a lot different than the wish. A dog, and particularly a puppy, is a *lot* of work and can turn your life upside down. Suddenly you have to rush home from work to walk it, or hire a dog walker, which is expensive. You can't leave for a weekend at the drop of a hat without figuring out what to do with the dog. And you can spend a lot of time walking, training, and cleaning up after it. They're not just cute, they're a lot of work. The reality may be more than a friend wants to cope with. But fools rush in where angels fear to tread, and I've cast my lot with the fools in the dog department, although I've gotten lucky with the end result. And I didn't actually "rush" into it, in most cases. I thought about it for a while and tried to be sure they really meant it when they said they wanted a dog.

A close friend of mine had a terrible bout of cancer and really went through the agonies of the damned, with fantastic results. She bravely faced the most aggressive treatments, and what was thought to be incurable cancer was cured in less than a year. It was truly a miracle, and I gave her a "miracle party" to celebrate her victory. For years she had said that she wanted a boxer, and with my heart in my throat, I decided to take her at her word. I found a good breeder and picked out a gorgeous dog for her, and the night of the party, I gave it to her. To say she looked stunned is a major understatement, and I'm sure as I gave it to her, she and her husband were thinking of the freedom they'd just lost. Their kids were grown, they love to travel, and having a dog at home was going to be a big change for them. I was terrified they'd refuse it, and instead they were both thrilled. They named the dog Miracle, she is now eight years old, and every chance they get, they tell me how much they love her. I was very lucky—it was just the right gift!! Looking back at some of the dogs I've given people, I don't know where I got the courage to do it. But something told me it was just right. I haven't done it often, but often enough to have potentially made some mistakes, but so far I haven't. That's a miracle in itself.

My next gift of a dog was equally brave, possibly even more so. A very, very dear friend, well into her eighties, had been struggling with cancer but was doing well. She was stable and seemed to have the situation in good control. She spent every

Thanksgiving with us, and that year she said more than once at dinner how much she wanted a dog. She had been "sharing" a dog with a friend who let her dog stay with her, and she said she was ready for her own.

My kids responded immediately as soon as my friend went home. "Mom, you have to get Isabella a dog!" I countered their pleas with reason—my friend wasn't young, she'd been sick, she had help but lived alone. And unlike my other friend, she didn't have a husband to help her with the dog. It seemed like a bad idea to me. My kids, who were all pretty much adults by then, insisted I had to give Isabella a dog. By that night they had convinced me, and on Monday morning I began a search for a dog. I still had misgivings about it, but my children wanted it to be a family gift from all of us, to this beloved friend who was practically a member of the family and was the godmother of one of my children. I figured that maybe my kids were smarter than I. And by the week before Christmas, what seemed like the right puppy had turned up. A small four-month-old Maltese, all fluffy and white. She was adorable when I saw her, and by then I knew my kids were right. All of the children were home for Christmas, and I could just imagine all of us presenting Isabella with the dog. She was going to be ecstatic (I hoped), and I came home to tell the kids, so we could plan to deliver the dog to her together. I ran into one of the kids as soon as I got home and told her I'd found Isabella's dog.

"Dog? What dog?" my daughter said, looking blank.

"You know, the dog you all wanted me to find for Isabella. I found her an adorable Maltese."

"Are you insane?" my daughter asked me. "She's too old for a dog, and she's sick. Why would you get her a dog?" My daughter looked at me as if I'd lost my mind, and I wondered if I had.

"You guys told me to get a dog for her, remember, after Thanksgiving dinner . . ."

"We never told you that." Had I imagined it? I went upstairs and found the others. It was unanimous. I was nuts. I had imagined it. And none of them would admit to thinking it was a brilliant idea a month before. (Kids are definitely more difficult than dogs.)

"Listen, guys, you told me to find her a dog. I did. You can deny it if you want. Now we have this dog, and I want you to come with me when we give it to her." By then I was sounding desperate, but not nearly as panicked as I felt. I'd been had. My sense of romance and fantasy had run away with me, and I had followed up on a suggestion none of them wanted to remember or to participate in now.

"We can't, we're busy." One of them had kickboxing, another had a Pilates class. My son had a big date with his girl-friend. The girls had manicures and pedicures scheduled. Not one of them would face the music with me, and I was stuck with this dog, and by then I was sure that Isabella would think I was even crazier than they did. I felt like a total idiot. I even called the breeder and warned her I might have to bring it back. I was sure the kids were right, and Isabella wouldn't want this dog. I went downstairs and had a long conversation with the dog, apologizing in advance for what I was sure was going to be a short visit to Isabella when she would look at me in horror and give me back the dog. Whose idea was this anyway, and why had I fallen for it?

I had gotten everything she could possibly need for the dog, gates, a playpen, blankets, Wee-Wee Pads, food, toys, bowls, collar, leash, just about everything but a driver's license and its own car. The dog came fully loaded, and I drove to my friend's house on Christmas Eve, with the dog looking mournfully at me. She looked like she was wondering how I'd gotten her into this, and I was asking myself the same thing. I was braced to have my loving, gracious friend throw the dog at me, or maybe slam the door in my face. Just as I had fantasized a happy reunion initially, I was imagining utter rejection on the drive to her house.

We arrived at her very respectable building, where the

doorman watched me unload the car, looking like a refugee, or at least like I was moving in, with my mountain of accessories for the dog. "Cute dog," he said, and I was ready to give her to him. I was almost too chicken to go upstairs with all the stuff, and the dog. He helped me get it all up to her apartment, and I took the dog in my arms and rang the doorbell with literally trembling knees. I felt like a complete jerk. "Hi Isabella, my kids told me to get you a dog, and now they think it's a terrible idea, so here it is. . . ." As I rang the bell, I could perfectly envision her refusing the dog and ushering me out. She had been a loving surrogate mother to me since I'd come to California thirty years before, as a young girl, long before I had my own family. Isabella had no children of her own and was a superior court judge until she retired. And with no children to visit her, it made the dog seem almost like a good idea. Almost, but not totally. I had no inkling how she'd react.

She came to the door to put me out of my misery at last. I knew she was having chemotherapy that day, which she was taking in stride, and had insisted she would be up to a visit at the appointed time. It was Christmas Eve. I looked at her sheepishly when she opened the door and smiled at me. "What's that?" she asked, as she saw the dog. I handed the little ball of white fluff to her and said, "She's yours. Merry

Christmas, Isabella, I got you a dog." It seemed pointless to remind her that she'd said she wanted one, since my kids didn't remember it either. Her eyes opened wide, and she took the dog from me immediately. She walked straight to a chair, put the dog on her lap, and began stroking her lovingly with a look of total bliss. The dog looked at me haughtily with an expression of "You can go now. I'm home."

My jaw nearly dropped. The dog never moved an inch off her lap, as Isabella beamed at me, and said, "I'm going to name her Trixie. That was the name of my first dog." By then I was crying, I was so happy, and Isabella truly looked like a kid at Christmas. Everything about the scene was exactly what Christmas should be—it was all about a kid and getting a puppy from Santa. I took out a disposable camera I had thought to put in my pocket, and took a roll of pictures of Isabella and Trixie, and then showed her all the equipment I'd brought. She looked amazed and pleased as she held Trixie in her arms. By then Trixie was ignoring me completely. I had served my purpose, and as far as Trixie was concerned, I'd been dismissed. And although she usually liked long visits, Isabella then walked me to the door, wished me a Merry Christmas, kissed me, and said "Thank you for my dog." And the next thing I knew, I was in the elevator laughing and smiling and crying. I had never seen anything so sweet in my life.

Isabella and Trixie: love at first sight
Danielle Steel

I don't think I'd ever seen Isabella so happy in thirty years. I drove home still smiling and was walking on air when I got home. She had just made Christmas for me. The crazy gift had been a smashing success. I told the kids about it, and they all shook their heads, unable to believe what I'd done.

It really was one of my best Christmases, just remembering the look on Isabella's face, and the dog looked as though she knew she belonged with her. And I expected to hear from Isabella the next day, letting me know about their first night together. But I didn't hear a word. Three days went by, and I got nervous, and knowing how polite Isabella was, I had the sinking feeling that maybe it was too much for her, and she was too embarrassed to complain. Puppies take time to settle in sometimes and can be difficult at first. Finally, I couldn't stand it, so I called. Isabella answered immediately, and I said I was wondering how things were going, and wanted to make sure she was okay and that the dog wasn't too much for her. She sounded instantly panicked and said, "No, no, we're fine. She's perfect. I love my dog. Goodbye." I wound up grinning all over again. Isabella was afraid that I was trying to take back her dog, which I surely wasn't.

A year and a half later, at the age of eighty-nine, Isabella watched a movie with her uncle in it. He was the famous actor Edward Everett Horton. Apparently she laughed a lot at the film, took a nap afterwards, and never woke up. I was deeply saddened at the loss of my friend but was so happy the dog had given her so much joy. And after they called to tell me, I wondered what would happen to Trixie and half-expected her family would ask me to take the dog back. Instead, they told me what a hard time they were having over Trixie, because everyone wanted the adorable dog Isabella had loved so much. Her friends and family were asking for her, and they finally gave Trixie to Isabella's brother, and she moved on to yet another adoring family and remained in good hands. It was the perfect end of the story and was surely the happiest gift I had ever given anyone. When I think of Isabella now, I think of that incredible Christmas Eve. I still have some of the photographs (I framed most of them for Isabella), with Isabella beaming and Trixie happily sitting on her knees. It personified Christmas for me, and I will never forget that day, or how terrified I was!

You would think that my jangled nerves over the gift to Isabella would have cured me, despite the happy end result, but it didn't. When my son lost his beloved childhood dog, Annabelle, I waited seven months while he mourned her, and although he said he would never have another dog, it made my heart ache to know how much he missed her (she had gone everywhere with him for fourteen years. He had gotten her when he was ten). And I succumbed to my own instincts and got him a Boston bull puppy for his birthday, the sweetest little puppy. She was much smaller than Annabelle and looked very different, which I thought was a good thing, and the breed suited him so well, and the whole family said I was out of my mind. He was shocked when he first saw her and spent a tough night wrestling with his sense of loyalty to the dog he had loved so much and lost. I kept the puppy while he thought about it, and the next day he called to claim her, and they have been inseparable ever since. Her name is Nancy, and she is irresistible and so loving.

And my last brave gift was this past Christmas. Once again I wrestled with the decision, but my ex-husband had been ill for many months, his ridgeback died a few years ago, and he had said repeatedly how much he missed having a dog. That's a dangerous thing to say to me. I thought about it for several months and finally decided to do it. I got him a King Charles spaniel for Christmas, and once again with huge trepidation, I brought it to him. He's a man, and when feeling well, he likes his freedom and to travel. I wasn't at all sure how he would respond to the gift, but once again he fell in love immediately. The puppy climbed into his lap, and he tells me constantly how perfect Perky is and how much he loves him. God smiled on me again on that one! I have to stop doing these things—

Maxx's new Boston bull,
Nancy, as a puppy
Cassio Alves

Perky, my gift to Tom

Robin Reynolds

Saukee, the Maltese I gave to
my friend Ginny after the one
she missed at auction

Cassio Alves

one of these days it could go wrong. But in all of these instances, it was the right thing to do, and I'm so glad I did.

My other experience "giving away" dogs (or in this case selling them for charity) was at our benefit for the foundation honoring my son Nick. Sadly, we lost my son Nicky at nineteen, and in his honor established a foundation to fund organizations that provide treatment and therapy for people with mental illness. And every two years, we gave a gala benefit to raise money. We called it the Star Ball. The benefit was a major event to coordinate, with six hundred and fifty guests who paid a fortune for tickets. We had stars who attended, always an important musical act (Elton John the last time), dinner, dancing, and an auction (of jewels, trips, cars, and some very exciting items). We discovered at our last two benefits that a fantastic way to raise money was to auction off a dog. We got two puppies the first time, and they were such a huge hit that we planned to auction three the last time. Two small dogs, and a large one (two Maltese and a boxer). A model would walk the puppies around all evening before the auction, and people went crazy for them and paid high prices for them. (They paid as much as twenty thousand dollars, for the benefit of the foundation of course, but they got to go home with a puppy. And another foundation I know of has auctioned puppies for as much as thirty-five thousand dollars.) The bidding was heated for both Maltese, and a beloved friend of mine was disappointed when she missed out on the Maltese puppy . . . so you guessed it, I gave her a Maltese puppy a few months later. I hear about her all the time and how much she loves her (Saukee). I lucked out again! (And a few months ago, light-years after Saukee, I gave her a second dog, also a Maltese, which she named Winni.)

And although the puppy auction was my favorite part of the benefit, it had its rocky moments. I loved watching the look of excitement on people's faces as they bid on a puppy they had been flirting with all night. Husbands and wives argued over the big dog (a Lab the first time) versus the small (a Yorkie or Maltese puppy), and real dog lovers were willing to go to any lengths and price for the dog they wanted. (As a side note, the benefit also auctioned me off for dinner. And the dogs went for a higher price! Go figure!)

We always chose the dogs carefully from reliable sources to make sure they were healthy. On the day of our last benefit, while I was checking the lighting, tables, sound, and room, hours before the ball, I got a frantic call from an assistant to tell me that the boxer we were auctioning off that night had diarrhea. "What should we do?" What should we do? Were they kidding? How did I know? Put a cork in her maybe? I said to call a vet, but I also made an immediate decision. I was not

Saukee and Winni
Virginia Harris

Ginny, with Saukee and Winni
Reed Harris

Nicky, the beautiful boxer we did not auction
(because of tummy problems)
Cassio Alves

going to auction off a sick dog. It could have been nothing, or it could have been a sign that she was more seriously sick. I didn't want to risk our thus-far-impeccable reputation on a sick dog. And we stuck to that decision. We didn't auction off the boxer, waited a week to make sure she was fine, had her checked out by the vet again, and gave her to a local San Francisco chef we knew and loved who wanted her desperately, and he was thrilled. (He named her Nicky.) She is still his beloved dog today. So all's well that ends well.

I don't know if I'd recommend giving a dog as a gift, it's a scary thing to do, and you have to know the recipient well, and how seriously they want a dog. But when it's the right thing to do, there is nothing better and nothing sweeter than seeing the sheer joy on someone's face when you give them a dog. I don't know if I'll ever do it again, but I cherish the memories of those I have given, and of how happy my friends and children were when they got them. It was really a blessing for them, and for me, and one that continues to bless for so many, many years.

Maxx's beloved Annabelle
Cassio Alves

SEVEN

In Loving Memory

There are endings and beginnings in life, new chapters, and old ones we remember fondly, with great tenderness. We don't "replace" those we love, whether dogs or people—they remain part of our history. But new people and dogs come into our lives and add excitement and joy and help us live new chapters.

For those who have loved a pet for many years, or even a shorter time, losing that pet can be incredibly sad. They fill a big space in our hearts, and leave a huge hole when they leave. And it's not uncommon to see some brave, strong man cry over his lost dog. We all do.

Dogs don't live as long as people, so it is inevitable that no matter how much we love them, or how well we care for them, we will lose them one day. Some breeds are longer-lived than others (notably dachshunds and Chihuahuas, and some terriers), which is something to consider. Small dogs almost always outlive big ones. Few big dogs live longer than ten or twelve years, while small dogs can make it to fifteen or sixteen, or even nineteen or twenty. And a few breeds are "heartbreak dogs," notoriously English bulldogs and Great Danes, who frequently die young.

I lost my first two black miniature Brussels griffons, Greta and Cookie, at thirteen. They were littermates and died within a few short months of each other. And their third sister died within weeks of them. They just ran out of gas and died peacefully, Greta of a heart attack in her sleep, and Cookie also in her sleep after a short illness. Both were fine until shortly before they died, and then they went straight downhill. There was no decision for us to make. Nature decided it for us—they were gone, and much missed. Cookie put on a good show till the end, but once she got sick, she declined rapidly. At times she seemed just too sick to hold on to any longer. We had to give her water and hand-feed her, and she could barely move, after a stroke. The vet had told us to get ready and bring her in whenever we felt the time was right. I finally decided that it wasn't fair to keep her going any longer, so I made the three-block drive to the vet with a heavy heart, planning to end her misery. She perked up the minute we got there, looked around with suspicion, and practically jumped out of my arms when the vet walked in. She hopped all over the place and danced around and would have tap-danced if she could, with a look that said, "Me? I'm fine! Don't be ridiculous! Just kidding!" The vet said she appeared to be doing great and sent us home, and I felt like an idiot. She pulled the same stunt two more times. She had no intention of going out under anyone's steam but her own and died quietly one night in her sleep. But she had no desire to let us make the decision for her!

We also lost my mother-in-law's dog, Trixie, who lived with us for seven years after my mother-in-law passed away. As I've said, she was a big brown standard dachshund and a particularly uncharming dog. And lived forever, until she died peacefully at twenty-one. We didn't realize at the time how our youngest daughter perceived that event. She was in nursery school, and at show and tell that day, she announced to her class that her daddy had put the dog in a box, buried it, and then it died. When I picked her up at school that afternoon, the teacher told me that I might want to straighten her out on the order of how things had happened, that the dog died and John buried her, not that she died as a result of being buried. It's interesting how kids view things!

My oldest daughter's Norwich terrier, Jack, was also very long-lived (the one who loved bubble gum and candy). He lived to be about nineteen and finally just wore out. He spent his last few days with me, sleeping in my bed, so I could watch him closely, while my daughter went to work. He was so frail by then that she didn't want to leave him alone, so I kept him with me. Jack and I had had a civil relationship for his nineteen years, but he was an independent sort, mostly attached to her, and he and I never really got closely connected. And as he lay in bed dozing on his last days, I saw him look up at me and panic. He looked like he was saying, "Oh sh--, this must be *really* bad if I'm with *her*!" Sadly, he lingered, and the vet finally said that it would be kinder to euthanize him. It's a decision my daughter had to make with her next dog as well, and I ached for her over the agonizing choice she was faced with. We've never had to make that decision with any of our other dogs, and it was a very, very hard one to make. But sometimes it's the right one. There are different ways to handle the process. There are vets who will come to your house now, to do it at home, if you prefer it. But any way or place you do it, it's a tough decision. And I've just learned that there is hospice for dogs now too. I hope it never comes to that for any of your dogs, or mine.

And even in sad moments, our family seems to create comic situations inadvertently. John and I promised to bury Jack in our garden, so my daughter didn't have to deal with that sad task. John dug a hole, only to discover when we went to bury Jack in a wooden box that our very old houseman had filled the hole with water from the hose (nearly creating a mudslide into our neighbors' garden), and there was no way to bury the dog, as the box floated on the water. John frantically bailed water before my daughter got home. We just got the job done when she appeared, while John stood there soaked, trying to look casual, and told her he'd been repairing a broken sprinkler. She never knew what had happened, but I still remember the hole filled with water and John frantically bailing, while we tried to bury her dog before she got home.

Even when we lose our pets in the appropriate span of time, it is never easy and always seems too soon.

My daughter Sam lost her childhood dog, a black miniature dachshund, Mia, who reached the end of her life at fourteen. As dachshunds are prone to, in the last few months of her life, she developed severe back trouble and lost the use of her back legs. We lovingly drove her home from L.A. to San Francisco to help nurse her, and she had everything from steroids to acupuncture and improved remarkably. She could walk again! And she finally seemed well enough to go back to Sam. I was planning to drive Mia back to L.A. after well over a month with me, and Sam was jubilant at having Mia come home and at how well she was doing. And then Mia played a final trick on me. All the plans were set for the drive to L.A.

the next day, with the vet's approval, and that night, hours before her triumphant return to L.A. (which seemed miraculous given the shape she'd been in two months before), Mia died quietly in her sleep. I couldn't believe it and was bereft for Sam. I drove to L.A. the next day anyway, and instead of handing Mia over to Sam, I had the unhappy task of telling Sam the bad news. But I wanted to tell her face to face, so I could put my arms around her and hold her when I told her. It was a terrible loss to Sam, but fortunately she still had Chiquita, the sixteen-year-old Chihuahua who had moved from New York to live with her. But we will always miss, love, and remember Mia.

The same thing occurred when my son Maxx lost his Boston bull Annabelle, also of his childhood. She was in perfect health and never showed her age, at fourteen. She acted like a puppy, and two days before he was to leave town and join me in France, Annabelle fell gravely ill in a matter of minutes. There was no warning, no slow winding down to prepare him. She went from fine to critical condition within five minutes, with seizures. He literally flew down the hill with her in his arms, the few blocks to the vet, shocked and panicked. He spent twenty-four hours at the pet hospital with her, never leaving her side, as I got hourly reports from him in France. And much to our relief, she improved enough for him to feel

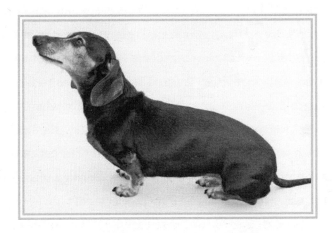

Sam's dog Mia (the chocolate eater) at thirteen
Cassio Alves

comfortable leaving. There was no explanation for the seizures, except possibly her age. She appeared to be on the road
to recovery. He spent a few more hours with her before he left,
fed her, and held her, and he had made me promise that I
would check on her through the night by phone from Paris,
while he was on the plane, so I could report to him when he
arrived. And once again Nature made the decision for us. Literally, as his plane took off from San Francisco, Annabelle
went to sleep peacefully and never woke up. He called as soon
as the plane touched down on the runway. The vet called to
tell me immediately, but I lied to Maxx when he landed and
called me. I couldn't bear telling him news like that over the
phone, and it nearly broke my heart to tell him when he got
home to the apartment. The loss was devastating. Annabelle
had been his shadow and beloved friend for fourteen years.
There is no replacing the companions of our childhood.

I think too, like losing a person we have loved, that losses
bring up other losses in our lives, and remind us of them, and
hit us hard. I will never forget how sad Maxx was to lose his
boyhood dog. (And Sam when she lost first Mia, and later
Chiquita.) Annabelle and Chiquita were probably our sweetest, most loving dogs.

Maxx grieved Annabelle terribly for the next many
months, and finally I gave him the Boston bull puppy that

put balm on his heart and whom he loves dearly. Annabelle will always be the boyhood dog he adored, but I'm happy to see that there is room in his heart for Nancy too.

Losing a pet can happen peacefully or in a more traumatic way. Some animals (and people) wind down over time, and you see them show all the signs of their age, and where things are headed. And sometimes they seem to be doing so well that they take you by surprise when things take a sudden turn for the worse. If they seem to be deteriorating slowly, you have the benefit of time to prepare you. And sometimes how well they appear can be deceptive. Twice now we have been fooled by unusually spunky old dogs who literally fell apart within hours, which is much harder to adjust to, and traumatic for their owners, who just didn't see it coming. (Again as can happen with people. My incredibly lively grandmother died almost instantly, while running between appointments and very busy with the joys of life. Although she died at an appropriate age, nearly eighty, her energy level, and how full of life she was, led us to believe she would live forever, and we were stunned by her sudden passing. The same happened with my ex-husband's grandfather, who lived to be 103 and still had all his faculties, was very sharp, and went to the office every day. He was a remarkable person, and I think we also came to believe he was eternal. But mortality catches up with

Chiquita at fifteen, still smiling!
Samantha Traina

all of us eventually. Old people and dogs can fool you if they still have a lot of energy and are in good health.)

We experienced that with my daughter Sam's second dog, Chiquita, two years after she lost Mia. Chiquita was sixteen by then, and full of bounce and energy. I loved watching her trot down the hall when she came to visit me. A vet we took her to guessed her age at eleven or twelve, when she was actually sixteen. Chihuahuas are notoriously long-lived, sometimes until twenty, and often until eighteen or nineteen. She was in perfect health, except for cataracts that became a problem two weeks before she died, and didn't bother her until then.

On a Sunday, she was fine, running up and down the hall, visiting everyone, and having fun. She and Sam were staying at my home, and we always enjoyed visits from Chiquita, she had no other health problems other than her eyes, and that was very recent. And on Monday morning she woke up and seemed ill, didn't eat, and was confused and a little dazed. She'd had a full checkup only days before and had a clean bill of health, appropriate to a dog half her age. We took her to the vet that Monday morning, assuming it was something minor, but being careful because of her age.

By lunchtime they called and said she was not doing well. She was having symptoms of a neurological problem, and her kidneys were not functioning well. And for the next thirty hours, she slid downhill so fast we didn't know what hit us. Mercifully her kidneys failing put her in a dazed state, so she wasn't suffering. And all our vets were hopeful that the situation would turn around. There was no warning of this sudden failure of her bodily systems, and by the next day she was in extremis, and thirty-two hours after the first sign of the problem, she was gone. We were all in shock, and poor Sam was devastated. The good news was that she didn't suffer, and I suppose it's better when people and dogs die quickly, don't linger in poor health for a long time, but when it happens like that, there is no time for those of us who love them to prepare. One minute they're fine, and the next minute they're gone, and we are bereft. It was a hard blow for Sam, who loved her so much and assumed she had a few good years left in her, given how healthy she was.

Chiquita's death also brought up some issues that pet owners sometimes have to deal with. At sixteen, a great age for a dog, sometimes medical personnel can put up less of a fight to save them, and are more inclined to let nature take its course, and let them go. She got the very best medical care possible at the hospital we took her to, but the possibility of putting her to sleep came up more quickly than it might have if she were younger. My theory was, and always is, that if she

*Chiquita (left) and Mia (right) when
they were dignified grandes dames*

Cassio Alves

wasn't suffering (and she wasn't), there was no need to rush to that decision. Euthanizing a dog is always an option. And saving a dog's life can be costly, and an expense some people may not want to undertake, or aren't able to. We wanted to fight for Chiquita's life right till the last minute, and I didn't like the suggestion of putting her to sleep. I wanted to give her a chance to rally, and so did Sam. The vets at the hospital co-operated with us.

But things went downhill so quickly that Chiquita died while Sam was rushing to the hospital to see her, having left work to do so. She was working in another city that day and had to get home in a hurry and take a flight to get there, and Chiquita died as the plane landed. Chiquita was so out of it by then that she wouldn't have recognized Sam anyway. But arriving at the hospital to see a very sick dog, and instead finding one that had just passed away, was traumatic and devastating for Sam. Life happens that way sometimes, and no matter how much we wish we could, we just can't control timing. Losing Chiquita so quickly, even at sixteen, was a shock for my daughter, and for all of us. She was such an adorable little dog. And you just don't know when life will turn on a dime and everything changes in the blink of an eye. But it was a blessing for the dog that she was only sick for two days, and she didn't suffer. We're grateful for that, although we will always miss her.

Like loving a person, loving a dog can eventually lead to heartbreak, but without question it's worth it.

Even if you lose a pet you love, think of getting another one, after the appropriate amount of time for you. Don't deprive yourself of that kind of love and joy in your life. We lose people we love, and we have to be able to go on without them, no matter how difficult that is at times. You have to be able to open your heart again, or a piece of you will die with them, and that's never a good thing. No matter how much we loved them, we have to cherish the memories, laugh at the fun we had, and love again.

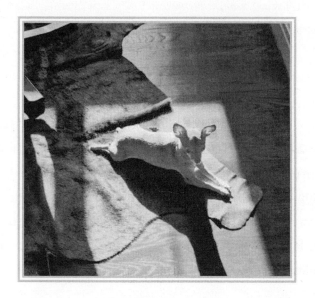

Tallulah

Victoria Traina

EIGHT

A Sibling for Your Dog?

I'm probably not the right one to write about this, considering the fact that I have nine children, and restraint has never really been my style. "Less is more" has never resonated for me, and "More is more" makes more sense. In terms of my children that theory worked out really well. And with eleven dogs and a pig at our very outrageous maximum, my perspective may be somewhat different than most.

It all depends on what you feel you can cope with, what you can afford, what your comfort level is, and then there is the love factor too. I would have regretted it forever if I had walked away from Minnie that day. She would have haunted me, and I'm so glad I was unable to resist her. We were meant to be together.

Sometimes I have a tendency to take on more dogs than I should—my soft heart does me in. The favorite griff I have now, Gracie, looked so sad as an "only dog," and I really thought she needed a friend after my other two griffs died of old age. I was going to get one, but two came up for adoption at the same time, and Brussels griffons are somewhat rare, and I ended up adopting both of them within weeks of each other. And then a year later a beautiful red griff came available and I bought her, so suddenly I had four. Hope and Meg, the two I adopted, are not as exceptional and are in the "Alice" category, as I mentioned earlier. They're really nice dogs but don't have outstanding personalities. Or maybe they would be better on their own or in a smaller group. Gracie and Ruby would be easier and more manageable on their own. But here I am trying to do right by all of them, and they have good lives, and are well loved and cared for when I'm away. But now Minnie has my heart, and is one of those very special dogs that you fall in love with a few times in a lifetime, like Greta and Gracie, and the pug I had as a child. But I will admit that there are times when I wish I had three dogs, instead of five, when I am trying to spend time with them.

Worse yet, only yesterday a pet shop I know in Paris, one that specializes in Chihuahuas and Yorkies, sent me photographs of a long-haired white teacup Chihuahua puppy, not quite as pretty as Minnie, but she was very sweet. I spent the day agonizing about it, severely tempted (she was so little and so cute), thinking about how hard or easy it would be to travel with a second dog. (According to my daughters, it's not easy traveling with two dogs. I've never done it.) And would it be more fun for Minnie to have a little friend, or would it upset her, and is she happier alone? It's hard to know, and I didn't want to commit to a dog long distance without spending time with her. And what if having her around turned Minnie into a dog, like Elmer the Basset, after the arrival of Maude? Those things are hard to predict. As I mulled it over, I could already see myself with a second Chihuahua. Finally, torn in all directions, I called my vet in Paris, and for a variety of reasons, he advised me against it, and I was off the hook, and said no. Some of us just can't resist a dog in need, or a puppy, and I seem to be one of those.

You can't guess how your existing dog will react to a new dog in the house. In most cases they adjust, but not always. Sometimes it simply doesn't work.

My daughter Victoria moved to New York with her Chihuahua and got a second one. And the first one, Chiquita, liked neither their New York apartment nor her new sibling, Tallulah, and my daughter was suddenly constantly refereeing between two warring dogs, one of whom was sulking over her new home, and Victoria felt severely torn between the two. Her older sister Samantha offered to step into the breach and babysit Chiquita for a while. (We all babysit each other's dogs if the dogs are sick, or their owners have to travel.) So Sam took Chiquita to L.A., and don't ask me why, but Chiquita absolutely loved it, was ecstatically happy, and got on perfectly with Sam's miniature dachshund, Mia. It was again one of those matches meant to be made. I'm sure Victoria missed Chiquita, but she saw her often at family events, and Chiquita was so happy with Sam that she moved in and stayed. And she and Sam were inseparable for the rest of Chiquita's life. She lived more than a decade with Sam. It was a switch that really worked, for both owners and the dog. And Victoria's Tallulah was much happier as an only dog. Sometimes, as an owner, you have to make a sacrifice for the well-being of the dog. Some dogs don't do well in groups or with a "sibling."

My son Maxx was faced with a difficult sibling situation too. He had his beloved Boston bull terrier, Annabelle, who was his shadow and went everywhere with him. Although she had boundless energy, she was still of a certain age, and had her habits and routine as an "only dog." Trouble started when he got an English bulldog puppy, who had all the exuberance and energy of the puppy she was, and the subtlety of a Sherman tank with her powerful bulldog body. She was physically much bigger, tougher, and stronger than Annabelle, even as a puppy. And she drove Annabelle totally nuts, leaping on her, tugging at her face, pushing her off the bed, and when all else failed, lying on top of her slobbering on her and playing rough. Annabelle looked as though she had been sentenced to torture. Nowhere that Annabelle went to hide from her was safe. The bulldog would find her, leap on her, and want to play some more. Annabelle looked like an old lady being mugged on the subway by a juvenile delinquent. The trainer who tried to calm the bulldog finally told my son that if he wanted to give Annabelle a miserable old age, he could keep the bulldog, but out of respect for Annabelle and her long years with him, she advised giving the bulldog puppy away. Annabelle could not adjust to a sibling. It was a hard decision, and he really enjoyed the funny bulldog he had named Noelle. But he loved Annabelle unreservedly, didn't want her to be unhappy, and she really was no match for Noelle, who meant her no harm but seemed like she was going to "play her to death." Maxx bravely searched for another home for the English bulldog puppy, with the help of the trainer. She moved on to a family that had a male bulldog who looked like her twin, and had the same energy level—he was named Meatball. Meatball and his family seemed perfect for Noelle, and they got on famously and have since grown up together. The right match for the dog was made, although a sacrifice for Maxx. I was very proud of him for doing the right thing for both dogs, Annabelle and Noelle.

Love in any form is a crapshoot, whether with people or dogs. People change, or turn out not to be what you expected, and sometimes so do dogs. If you buy a puppy, you can't tell what it will be like as an adult dog, or be sure what its personality will be. And if you adopt an adult dog, you may find you have a gem, or you could wind up with problems created by someone else. It's good to try and find out why the owner is giving them up. Because they're moving away or have health problems themselves, or is there something wrong with the dog? Rescue dogs can be wonderful, but some have issues too, particularly if they were abandoned or abused.

Obviously, I miss having children around me and devoting my life to them. My life is very different now that my children have grown up, even with one still at home. There are different chapters in our lives. And in these current chapters, I have more time for me. For years, I was too busy to read magazines, never had lunch with friends, didn't go to the hairdresser. I was either taking care of kids, or my husband, or writing books. Now I have time to do the things I haven't done for years, and sometimes it's actually fun.

And at this point in my life, I have time for dogs. So probably taking on another dog doesn't seem daunting to me. For a woman with nine kids, how scary can two Chihuahuas be? But would another dog be good for Minnie? Particularly one of her own size and breed. Dogs instinctively gravitate to dogs of their same breed. Right now I decided no, but if I fell in love with another one, would I be able to resist? Maybe not. I don't know. Or maybe reason would prevail. It is certainly easier traveling with one dog. And Minnie is so used to being the center of attention now, I'm not sure how well she would adjust. I have a feeling that Minnie likes being an "only" dog.

For now Miss Minnie is a little princess, happily getting spoiled, with her Paris wardrobe and everyone doting on her. Maybe I will get another Chihuahua one day, but not now. And if I did, just like with Minnie, I would have to fall in love. (It was a sign of major maturity and restraint that I turned down the puppy I was offered yesterday.) I never expected to, but I find I really like this breed. They're tiny, but they're hardy and spunky and have wonderful personalities. And they're very smart. I suspect some may be barky, but Minnie hardly ever barks, which I like—except at the fax machine.

I think, as with anything else, you need to know how much you can take on. Can you afford a second dog? Do you want to? Dogs can be expensive in today's world, grooming, boarding if you go away, their basic needs, and the vet for checkups, vaccinations, and particularly if they get sick. Do you have the time and energy for another dog? I have enough of both for another dog—that doesn't mean it's right, but I know I could manage it, which leads me into deep waters at times.

Sometimes the decision about whether to get a second dog is decided by the breed. Dogs of some breeds do better on their own, while others are one-man dogs and would be seriously unhappy to have a rival for your attention. Or it could make your first dog aggressive or depressed. Certain breeds have known traits, which it's worth learning about. Years ago I almost adopted a dog whom my vet advised me was of a breed that would almost certainly try to kill my other dogs. Needless to say, I didn't adopt him. So you really do need to know about the breed and how they respond to other dogs. And to children, if you have kids. Some breeds are more child-friendly than others.

Minnie seems ecstatically happy on her own. She is one happy little dog, and everyone in her entourage adores her, and she knows it. She has a terrific life. Griffs are known to be happy in pairs or more and seem happy with each other, like my four Griffs. They seem content to be in a "pack." But for now, Minnie is more of an only child.

So I have to leave your decision of a second or third dog

up to your own wisdom and knowledge of yourself and your circumstances. I'm sure you'll make the right decision. After you weigh the pros and cons, listen to your heart. But if you want advice about whether to have a ninth child, be sure to call me (and the answer will be yes!). As for a second or third dog—that's up to you.

Nick's beloved dog Molly
J. M. Reed

NINE

Irreconcilable Differences.

It Happens.

Dogs have personalities, just like people, and sometimes when an adorable puppy grows up, the adult dog they turn into just isn't a match with us. Or they have some really unfortunate trait that makes living with them from difficult to impossible.

It helps to know the traits of the breed—they may not always hold true, but often they do. And being well informed about the breed you're buying, or finding out from a breeder if possible what the personalities of the parents of the puppy are like, can be important. In a world where romantic relationships can be a challenge, sometimes a successful match with your dog as it grows up can be challenging or disappointing too. And when that happens, then what? What do you do?

We've had some dog mismatches in our family, which ranged from the ridiculous to the tragic, in one case. The most obvious reason for a mismatch is if a dog is dangerous in some way, either to you or to your kids, or even to others, but most mismatches aren't that extreme. Some can be worked out and some just can't, again like people. There are some people you can spend a week on vacation with, or a weekend, and hope you never see them again. Some dogs leave you feeling that way too. Or sometimes a dog can work out well and then no longer be the right fit when circumstances in the family change.

My beloved basset Elmer turned out to be one of those in the long run. As I mentioned earlier, once Maude joined us, he was a lot doggier and a lot less fun. And I kept them both for years. But once I had a baby in the house again, the combination just didn't work. A basset hound is essentially a big dog on very short legs, which puts them face to face with a very small child. Elmer was a seventy-pound dog, with big jaws and big teeth, and a sweet nature. He paid no attention to the baby when it came along, but once my son was walking around the kitchen at a year old, and waving a slice of salami or bologna in Elmer's face, he was not quite as sweet and would snatch it from the toddler's hand in one gulp, something like *Jaws*. And it turned out Maude never liked kids and had tried to bite more than one. So it became dangerous to have them in the house with a toddler. And we found a home for them in the country with a family with older kids. It worked out well for all concerned, Elmer and Maude were happy there, and I was relieved. No mishap had taken place, but it could have easily.

For a very brief time, I also had a rescue dog, a black Labrador named Betsey, who was friendly and exuberant and loved everyone. *Exuberant* was the operative word. She had some kind of latent, or not so latent, hunting gene, and her greatest thrill was spotting my then five-year-old daughter, wagging her tail furiously, and then leaping on her and pinning her to the ground, barking ecstatically, showing me what she'd "caught," and keeping my daughter there, facedown, until I arrived to congratulate Betsey on her prize. I couldn't break her of the habit, even after countless friendly introductions to my daughter, who wasn't terrified of her but got tired of lying facedown on the ground while Betsey stood on her and barked with glee. I decided to give up early and found the Lab another home quickly, before we got attached to her, and once again it was a home with older kids, not young ones. She couldn't knock them down!

Sometimes a dog can be wonderful but just not a match for you, in terms of their habits and needs. And some dogs do better on their own, while others are happy in a group of other dogs. Once again like people, some are loners or meant to be only children, while others are more sociable and team players. At one point we got a beautiful white Maltese, who had a sweet disposition and made it clear that she did not like being part of a group of dogs. She had unlimited energy. In fact, she was turbocharged and had a lot in common with the Energizer Bunny. To make her feel special, and give her some extra attention and alone time, I would keep her in my office, on her own, while I was writing. My other dogs, when given that opportunity, would look at me with drooping eyelids and, deciding that it was all very boring, in ten minutes or less were sound asleep. I had named the little Maltese Faith, and my hours of typing only seemed to rev her engines to an alarming degree. She would start out on jet speed and get busier and wilder through the day. First she'd chew through all the electrical wires. Then she'd wipe out the phone. After that, she'd bounce around the furniture, gnawing cushions, make a bold stretch toward the bookcase and eat my books. After that, she'd nibble on my toes, usually eat at least one of my shoes, dance around to show me how cute she was, and bark at every sound. And yes, she was very cute, but after fourteen hours of typing, I'd be starting to sag in my chair, and Faith would still be looking for things to do. She was tireless, too much so for me. No matter what I did, I couldn't wear her out, and when I sent her back to play with the other dogs, she looked unhappy. And in my office, she was distracting, and a nightmare. It took me several months to finally admit we were mismatched. I needed a dog with less energy (a *lot* less!), and I strongly suspected she needed to be an only child.

A friend of mine had lost her dog around that time and was heartbroken, missing her dog. And I think it was a Maltese too. I talked to her honestly about my experiences with Faith, that she was clearly a great dog but had too much energy for me and maybe needed to be an only dog. My friend came to meet her, and it was love at first sight. I knew the minute I saw them together that it was right. Faith went to spend a few days with her, and their romance flourished and has only deepened over time. Faith moved on to her new home, and I've run into my beaming friend with Faith a few times. I really guessed that one right. I've always liked a slightly ragtag look to my dogs, with tousled hair, and not all impeccably groomed and clipped. But once Faith made it to her new home, her beautiful white Maltese hair was perfectly brushed. She was wearing a pink rhinestone-studded collar and leash, and when I saw her, she gave me a look that clearly said she had risen in the world and had no use for a commoner like me. She had become a princess. She strutted proudly beside her new owner, while my friend told me all the things they'd been doing together. They were an absolutely perfect match. Faith and I never were, and I'm so happy that I had the courage to say so and let her be much happier somewhere else. She never did anything "bad," she just wasn't right for me.

We had one very, very bad experience with a French bulldog I brought back from Paris, named Sophie. Some people are nice, others aren't, and dogs are much the same. And some people (and dogs) are simply insane. Sophie was insane. (I wasn't so sure about the breeder I got her from either, since he told me a few months later that a fortune teller had told him I was his long-lost mother and I should adopt him immediately. P.S., I didn't). In any case, Sophie flung herself at anyone who walked by, barking ferociously, wanting to attack them. And the mistake I'd made in getting her came to a tragic end, when she attacked and killed the very old Brussels griffon we had, who had belonged to my late son Nick. The loss was sad for all of us. Molly was old and blind and no match for Sophie, and it was over instantly. Sophie's partner in crime was Tommy, a male griffon I had who, unlike my others, had never been friendly and had bitten several people over the years, and we kept him anyway. They set on Molly together. I called our vet the day it happened, and we put up both Sophie and the male griffon for adoption and sent them away the same day they attacked Molly. I didn't want to see them again. We found good homes for both of them, where they did well separately, but after what they did, they didn't belong with us. Nothing like it has ever happened before or since. It was a sad episode in our dog life and a very sad end for Molly.

Less dramatic, we got another French bulldog a year or so later, who arrived with giardia, a contagious illness, and had to be isolated from the other dogs for five months, to avoid infecting them. Once released from quarantine, she showed signs of aggression, and we didn't want a repeat of the Sophie episode. Our vet adopted the French bulldog. And although many people love them, after those two experiences, I wouldn't get a French bulldog again, but that's just me. Others seem to do well with them.

We've adopted dogs successfully too, not just placed them with others. When Greta's breeder called to tell me that her littermate was being given up by her owner, because she (the owner) was ill and could no longer care for her, we took her immediately. Cookie spent ten happy years with us until she died at thirteen.

It's not always easy to make the right match when you buy a puppy, or guess who they will turn out to be once they're grown. It's a crapshoot, like anything else in life. You do your best to make it work, but if you can't, sometimes it's fairer to the dog, and everyone involved, to find a home and an owner who suits them better. Not all matches are made in heaven, and sometimes it works out right the second time around. And if you are going to place a dog in another home, it's best to be honest about what's not working well for you. It may even be your personality, not the dog's. Or just not the right fit. But hiding their problem traits, if they have any, will only create another mismatch. Even when we gave away Sophie and Tommy, we made full disclosure of what they'd done to my son's dog. Both went to homes where there were no other dogs, and they never had a problem, but their new owners knew what they were getting, and why they had been wrong for us. It's like in any relationship—being honest is essential.

In any case, if you seriously believe you have a mismatch on your hands, more than likely there is a person or a family out there who would be thrilled to have that dog, and where even the dog would be much happier than he or she is now. Sometimes "irreconcilable differences" happen in life, even with dogs. Don't beat yourself up over it, just try to find a solution that will work for all concerned.

Minnie in her hotel room
in New York, en route from Paris
to San Francisco
Victoria Traina

TEN

Minnie's Return from Paris

or

Long Trips

Personally, I don't like long, long plane trips. I'm not a fan of flying for twelve hours or longer, or facing huge time differences when I arrive. I'm lucky that I don't suffer from jet lag, and I've discovered that the secret to that, for me, is to break up long trips. So I don't fly over the Pole when traveling from San Francisco to Paris (which takes about twelve hours). I stop in New York for a night or two, which turns it into a five-hour trip and a six-hour one and gives me the added bonus of visiting with two of my daughters, who live in New York. Breaking the trip up that way is a total win-win for me and seems to avoid jet lag completely. It's a perfect solution, and as I prefer night flights, I sleep on both flights

(San Francisco to New York, and New York to Paris) and arrive fresh as a daisy. And those two short flights are easy for Minnie too. She wears herself out all day, has all her normal meals, and by the time we board a red-eye flight at ten or eleven p.m. or later, she just curls up in her bag and goes to sleep. And both the winds and time difference are in our favor.

But it's the return trip from Paris to New York that is a tough one. The flight is long, and nothing is in our favor, except the movies and a decent French meal, neither of which Minnie can enjoy. The winds are against you going west (from New York to California also, but that flight is shorter than the Paris–New York flight), and with rare exceptions, instead of six hours flying to Paris, it's about an eight-hour flight from Paris to New York, sometimes longer. Add to that two hours in security before the flight, and an hour waiting for bags and going through customs in New York, and it's an eleven-and-a-half- or twelve-hour adventure. And if the plane is really delayed, as happens often in today's world, it can be thirteen or fourteen hours. But twelve at best. It's one of the reasons, other than their size, that I never tried to take any of my Brussels griffons with me. I didn't want to undertake a twelve-hour trip with an adult dog that had never flown before. She might freak out or bark her way across the Atlantic (and someone might try to kill me!). In Minnie's case, she's grown up traveling and started flying at twelve weeks. And she's so tiny that she can move about comfortably in her carrying bag. My griffs would have been completely immobilized in the bag and couldn't even turn around. It always seemed cruel to me to try to take that long flight with them, so I never did— even if I could have put them on a diet and shaved off two pounds for the weight limit, which seemed mean too.

But even for tiny Minnie, twelve hours or longer in her traveling bag seems endless. She has weathered it well, but I can tell that she doesn't enjoy that leg of the trip, and who could blame her? And it's always a day flight, so she is confined at a time when she'd normally like to be running around.

I carefully consulted with the vet before the first time I made the return trip, and even the outward-bound flights, and had been told to give her water every two hours and feed her every four hours. When tiny dogs are very young, they can get hypoglycemic, so it's important to keep them fed and watered. We even have a tube of a vitamin meat paste, and I can put a little dab on my finger, and she loves it.

She's also very good about not peeing off her Wee-Wee Pad, or in confined spaces, and I was worried about her not going to the bathroom in her bag for so many hours. So on all the long Paris–New York flights, I take her to the bathroom in her carrying case, let her out, and put her on a Wee-Wee Pad. The theory is to let her move around freely for a few minutes. Great idea, but Minnie doesn't like it. She stands in the middle of the bathroom, on her Wee-Wee Pad, her legs stiff, and won't move an inch. She actually likes small, confined spaces, and I think feels safe there. Being let loose on the plane, in the bathroom, is frightening and not fun for her. She won't move, walk, or pee, she just stands there, staring at me. So it is a very long flight for her, but remarkably she does okay. Instinctively, she won't drink water, as though she knows she'd have to pee. But I offer water anyway, several times on every flight. I don't give her canned dog food, but I put kibble in a bowl in the bag, but she eats very little on the plane. I hear her crunch it occasionally. So we manage on the long flight, but I always feel sorry for her. It's a long trip even for me, and worse for her. I don't know what we'd do if the flight were longer. I think that's about as far as I'd take her. So we won't be flying to Australia anytime soon.

Amazingly, she seems to like her carrying bag that we use for the plane. I would think it makes her feel claustrophobic, but I think it's actually cozy for her. She often climbs into the bag, just for the fun of it, when we're at the hotel in New York, or even at home. And she pulled a disappearing act on me one time, when I looked everywhere in the hotel room for her and couldn't find her, and thought she'd run away when someone opened the door, and I found her happily asleep in her bag. As much as we travel, it's now a familiar world for her. And I have discovered that Chihuahuas like small spaces.

Years ago my daughter Victoria called me from New York in a panic. Her teacup Chihuahua had vanished. She had looked everywhere and couldn't find her, and she was terrified that she had either escaped the apartment or gotten stuck in a small space somewhere and been injured. She called the doorman of her building to ask if someone had seen her. I offered every helpful suggestion I could, and crying miserably over her lost Tallulah, Victoria blew her nose in a tissue, stepped on the garbage can pedal to toss away the tissue, and there, sound asleep, was Tallulah. She had gotten into the garbage can and gone to sleep. She has also hidden in open suitcases. They curl up and just happily go to sleep, while we frantically look for them.

To be sure that no one lets Minnie escape at the hotel, I always leave the Do Not Disturb sign on my door, so an unwitting or careless cleaning person doesn't leave a door open and let her run away. It just seems safer to keep strangers out when I'm not there. They might also try to pick her up and drop or hurt her without meaning to. She's hard to resist.

Chihuahuas are also adventurous and have been known to

take off and hit the road. One of Minnie's favorite games is to have me run around my desk about two hundred times until I catch her. She's a lot faster and more elusive than I am. (It's embarrassing to be outsmarted by a two-pound dog!)

Chiquita once escaped from our garden and happily trotted down the street for several blocks before we caught up to her. My other daughter's Chihuahua, Tallulah, slipped out of her collar, and my daughter ran at full speed in stilettos in New York traffic to catch her. And a friend's Chihuahua ran away while with a dogsitter and was missing for several days. (She was identified by the nail polish the groomer had put on her toes, since she made her getaway without her collar!)

Because of their size and proportionately tiny necks, which are fragile, all vets recommend harnesses for Chihuahuas instead of collars. And they can also slip out of their collars with an artful turn of the head. They can't slip out of a harness. So a harness is much safer for them, and reassuring for you. And you should keep your dog's ID tags on their collar or harness at all times.

In addition, in today's world of technology, many dog owners put a chip in their dog's shoulder (a vet can do it easily), and when taken to a vet and scanned, if lost, all your contact information is on the chip. Some owners have their dogs tattooed. And all dogs need license tags in any city, and many owners have personal ID tags on their collars, with their name and phone number on it.

Being a "belt and suspenders" kind of person, Minnie has an international chip, required for our travel into France, and an American one. She wears a tiny collar with an ID tag on it, and when I'm going to put a leash on her, she wears a harness with an ID tag. And her travel carrier has a tag on it too! I don't want to take any chances if she gets lost!

Mistaken identification of one's dog can be embarrassing, as it is with one's children. I once arrived late at a birthday party that one of my children was attending, saw my child from the back at the table eating birthday cake, swooped down on her and gave her an enormous hug of greeting while standing behind her (I could only see her blond hair, not her face), but I was sure it was my daughter and had no doubt. It was a loving, exuberant moment, except that it turned out not to be my child. I scared the poor unsuspecting (wrong) child half to death. She turned around to look at me midhug as though I was crazy. Oops. Sorry. Not my kid. My children are cursed genetically with a somewhat dubious sense of humor (at every age, almost from birth), so my own child was laughing her head off at my mistake, while watching me from across the table, as I hugged and kissed a stranger. It can happen with dogs too. (Children can be merciless and often enjoy it when their parents make fools of themselves. Dogs are more charitable about it, and at least don't laugh and point, and they don't tell their friends about it later. . . . "You should have seen my mom—" doing whatever stupid thing you did.)

And it can happen with dogs too. My daughter Victoria came to breakfast one morning, still half asleep, and encountered her dog in the kitchen. Victoria's fawn-colored Chihuahua Tallulah is very docile, affectionate, and sweet-natured. And as Victoria sat down to eat, her dog growled and barked fiercely at her, not pleased in the least to see her. Victoria looked shocked and upset, and when she reached down to pet her and pick her up, the dog fled and then cowered in the corner (the dog, not Victoria) and continued barking furiously. Victoria was stunned and said, "What's wrong with Tallulah?" Nothing. My youngest son's girlfriend has a Chihuahua of the same size and color. The dog didn't know us well then and at that time regarded us all with hostility and suspicion. (She likes us now.) The girlfriend's dog happened to be at the house that morning. And one of my other children observed the scene, laughed at Victoria, and said, "That's not your dog!!" Closer observation then confirmed that it was the visiting Regina, NOT Victoria's Tallulah. Oh. Oops. Regina eventually calmed down, and Victoria ate her breakfast looking a little sheepish, not to have recognized her own dog, in her sleepy state. It's always somewhat embarrassing when you don't recognize your own dogs or children. (I once tried to pet my neighbor's two dogs, being walked by a dog walker. As I reached down to them with a friendly greeting, one tried to bite me, while the other one happily lifted his leg on me. They turned out not to be my neighbor's dogs after all, but a stranger's dogs, of the same breed.) Try to look closely before hugging or petting children and dogs. The dog or child you are trying to embrace may not be your own. Just a friendly hint from one mother/dog owner to another.

And Minnie has her sneaky moments with her traveling bag too. She seems to consider it her home away from home, which is a good thing since she has to spend time in it when we travel. She never looks upset when I put her in it.

On a recent trip from Paris, after the twelve-hour trip (even I get cranky after such long travel, but she doesn't), she had an upset stomach. I called the Paris vet, who told me to use the cans of special diet food he'd given me for cases like that, but not give her any dry kibble. I followed his instructions to the letter. Canned food only, no dry food. Minnie usually likes to have a bowl of each twice a day. And when I gave her her dinner, she looked at me as though to say, "Excuse me, you forgot something." Sorry, Minnie. No kibble. She gobbled up the canned food, and a little while later, she disappeared. But this time I could see her. Her little bottom was sticking up in the air, her tail was wagging happily. She had dived into her carrying bag, where she remembered she still had a small bowl of dry kibble, which I had forgotten, but she didn't.

"Minnie!" I said in a slightly stern motherly tone, and she turned to look at me with totally false innocence, as though to say "Me? I'm not doing anything." Yeah, right. Try that one on someone else. She dove back into the bag, her tail still wagging, and I could hear her loudly crunching the kibble. Every now and then she would stop, give me that totally dishonest look of false innocence, and go back to crunching. I took the kibble away, but she was really funny about it. She slunk out of the bag with a look of "Oh, okay, if you're going to be that way about it." As usual, she had me laughing. She is very expressive, everything is written on that little white face, and in those big brown eyes. She has tiny little eyebrows that give her a permanent look of innocence and surprise. And she has a tiny little brown nose.

She's a good eater now, but sometimes she's a picky eater. Sometimes she's just not hungry, as we aren't, and makes up for it at the next meal or the next day. I no longer worry about it, although I did at first. I've since learned that Chihuahuas eat when they're hungry, and not just because the food is available, like some other breeds. In the beginning, when she didn't eat, I'd try to find ways to tempt her. I hand-fed her a few times, although they say you shouldn't spoil them—they'll learn quickly just how big a softie you are. (In my case, think marshmallow.) And my assistant, seeing me hand-feed her, scolded me and told me I would spoil her. "Who? Me?" Yeah, me. But I was worried that she'd missed a meal. (I discovered later that if I give her chew sticks to gnaw on, she won't eat later.) We were even though, because the next time I cruised through the kitchen, I found my assistant putting her food in the microwave to warm it. He loves her too and was just as worried she wasn't eating. And warmed food was going to spoil her just as surely as my hand-feeding her. She was giving him those Gypsy eyes that told him how mistreated she was, getting cold food straight out of a can. Now she eats on her own, with no help from me, and we don't warm her food. And she eats just fine.

You have to be careful with tiny stomachs too. My griffs have delicate stomachs (some breeds just do, while others are hardier) and always get sick when people feed them from the table. And the vet warned me that in Minnie's case, at two pounds, feeding her human food casually could really make her seriously sick or even kill her. He said that cheese, cold cuts/meats, or sweets like cookies or cakes could make her very, very ill. And, of course, chocolate, whether milk chocolate or dark, but especially dark, can kill a dog. They can't process it, need their stomachs pumped, and have to be given charcoal immediately. But chocolate can literally be a killer. Fortunately, that's not true for people since I'm a devoted chocoholic. But even what seem like harmless treats from the table can be nearly or actually lethal to a dog the size of Minnie. So well-meaning friends who want to give her a treat from the table are sternly warned off. And I recently learned that grapes can be fatal to a dog too.

Because Europeans are so loving with their dogs, they are much more casual about what they feed them, and they love giving them samples of what they eat themselves, anything from prosciutto to cooked meat and vegetables to bits of fruit. But in Minnie's case, it would make her very sick. I always watch my friends there like hawks so they don't give her something they consider a treat but would make her sick. They think it's neurotic of me, but I trust the vet on that one, and he is emphatic about it.

I guess dogs really do resemble their masters. I've never had a great stomach either. Stress of any kind always hits my stomach first. And travel sometimes does it to me too. The last time we flew to New York, the vet thought Minnie's upset stomach was due to the stress of the trip. Twelve hours in that bag on an airplane can't be easy. And for many years now I drink tap water only in San Francisco. Everywhere else I drink bottled water, because constantly changing water from the tap, in different cities around the world, wrecks my stomach. I give Minnie bottled water now too. It sounds extravagant, but she drinks very little, and why stress her stomach when we change cities so often? It's just simpler to make life easy for her, which in the end is easier for me too.

We learned an important lesson with Victoria's Chihuahua. She used to feed her cold cuts, because she was a picky eater too. And her Chihuahua got a hole in her stomach and was very sick for several months, frighteningly so, so now we are all very rigid about what we give them to eat and drink. Sorry, Minnie, no prosciutto or salami, no chocolate cake or cookies. What can I say? It's a dog's life.

Pure Joy
Stephanie Unger

ELEVEN

Pure Joy
or Why Not?

As I said earlier, I find that the answer to many things at this point in my life is "Why not?" I have spent a lifetime worrying about how what I do will impact other people. I have been a mother since I was nineteen, earlier than most. And I was a wife for thirty-six years, starting at seventeen. For all of that time, and even now, with adult kids, I've had to think about how what I did affected someone else. Was it good for them? Their needs had to come first, and I wanted it that way, and still do. I don't want the choices I make to adversely affect them or the common good. The family comes first, as I believe it should. Sometimes that means sacrifice, or giving up something you really want to do. But at this point in my life, I realize that some of it really doesn't matter. I no longer have to worry about embarrassing a child when I pick them up at school in Wellington boots, even if it's pouring rain. "Omigod, Mom, you can't wear those!" Yes, I can. I'm not going to wear stilettos in the rain, or get wet feet. "You're not going out in *that?*" is a mantra you hear often, if you have girls. And the answer now is "Yes, I am," if it makes me happy. I wouldn't do anything to hurt them or embarrass them publicly, but it's not going to kill anyone if I wear sandals they hate or a hairdo they don't like. And I don't have a husband who has to agree on whether or not I get a dog. And after so many years of pleasing and taking care of so many people, it's something of a shock to realize I can do whatever I like about some things, and certainly minor ones.

We all get into habits and travel familiar paths. There is something comforting about that. But it's also exciting to do new things, meet new people, see something I've always wanted to see, develop new passions, explore talents I didn't know I had. I've embarked on two additional careers in recent years, opening a gallery of contemporary art to show the work of emerging artists, and writing song lyrics, and it's truly exciting to learn and try something different. It's fascinating to open new doors, even if challenging at times. It makes the possibilities life offers suddenly limitless if I am willing to say "Why not?", and it begins to touch on every area of my life. The "I shoulds" begin to melt away, and the "I can't's" become fewer. I can't go to China because . . . I shouldn't have a dog, because . . . Suddenly I find it infinitely more exciting to say "Why not?" Why not go to that party or dinner, meet those people, take a trip, learn a language, start a painting even if I never painted before? And it brings new life to my work to stretch the boundaries and expand my horizons. It may startle those around me at first, and even threaten those who have known me for many years, particularly the people who are afraid to say "Why not?" themselves. Courage and newness can be frightening to other people. It alarms them when anyone breaks loose from the pack.

And allowing myself to love a dog, or even two or three dogs, may be part of that. I never thought I'd be a woman with a Chihuahua or be gaga over a dog. I have the time and the love to give, I can afford to feed her, and my children are all in good shape. I'm not hurting anyone by having a tiny little dog, or by buying her a rhinestone collar or a silly pink sweater with a teddy bear on it. She gives me endless joy, and she takes nothing away from anyone else. And life is about joy—it's about what makes us smile and feel good, and puts a spring in our step. If that tiny white face with the Yoda ears makes me laugh when I look at her, my life is happier, and my world a better place. Hard things happen to all of us, and have to me as well. We've all had our tough moments, our disappointments and heartbreaks, we've paid our dues. We've earned the right to be happy. We don't have to apologize for it. It's okay to feel good, or to laugh at a little dog or a big dog, or to fall in love with a funny, furry face. And that happiness seeps out of us like great smells from a bakery and touches those around us and makes them feel good too. Don't let anyone deprive you of that. You have a right to feel great, and to as much joy as you can get. And when Charles Schulz said "Happiness is a warm puppy," he knew what he was talking about. For me, for now, that's Minnie. Happiness is Minnie, hiding her kibble, and sliding across my kitchen floor in Paris to hide a toy before I can get it, and then looking back at me with that knowing look. She knows just how cute she is, and how much I love her. For me, happiness is a little white two-pound dog. Allow yourself the luxury of letting happiness be whatever it is to you. And for some of us, a puppy or a dog we love is pure joy. May that special joy find its way into your heart and keep you warm.

Miss Minnie in her favorite office chair in
San Francisco, across from my desk

Alessandro Calderano

ABOUT THE AUTHOR

DANIELLE STEEL has been hailed as one of the world's most popular authors, with over 600 million copies of her novels sold. Her many international bestsellers include *Winners, First Sight, Until the End of Time, The Sins of the Mother, Friends Forever, Betrayal, Hotel Vendôme, Happy Birthday, 44 Charles Street,* and other highly acclaimed novels. She is also the author of *His Bright Light,* the story of her son Nick Traina's life and death, and *A Gift of Hope,* a memoir of her work with the homeless. And she writes children's books, song lyrics, and poetry.

ABOUT MINNIE

MINNIE was born on August 26, 2011. She is a Virgo. She lives in Paris and San Francisco, and spends time in New York frequently. She is the owner of the author Danielle Steel.